HOLY PRAYING ANGELS COLORING BOOK
By Valeriia Laryoshyna

Copyright © 2023 by Valeriia Laryoshyna

First paperback edition May 2023

Book design by Valeriia Laryoshyna

ISBN: 9798394346170

Published by Kindle Direct Publishing

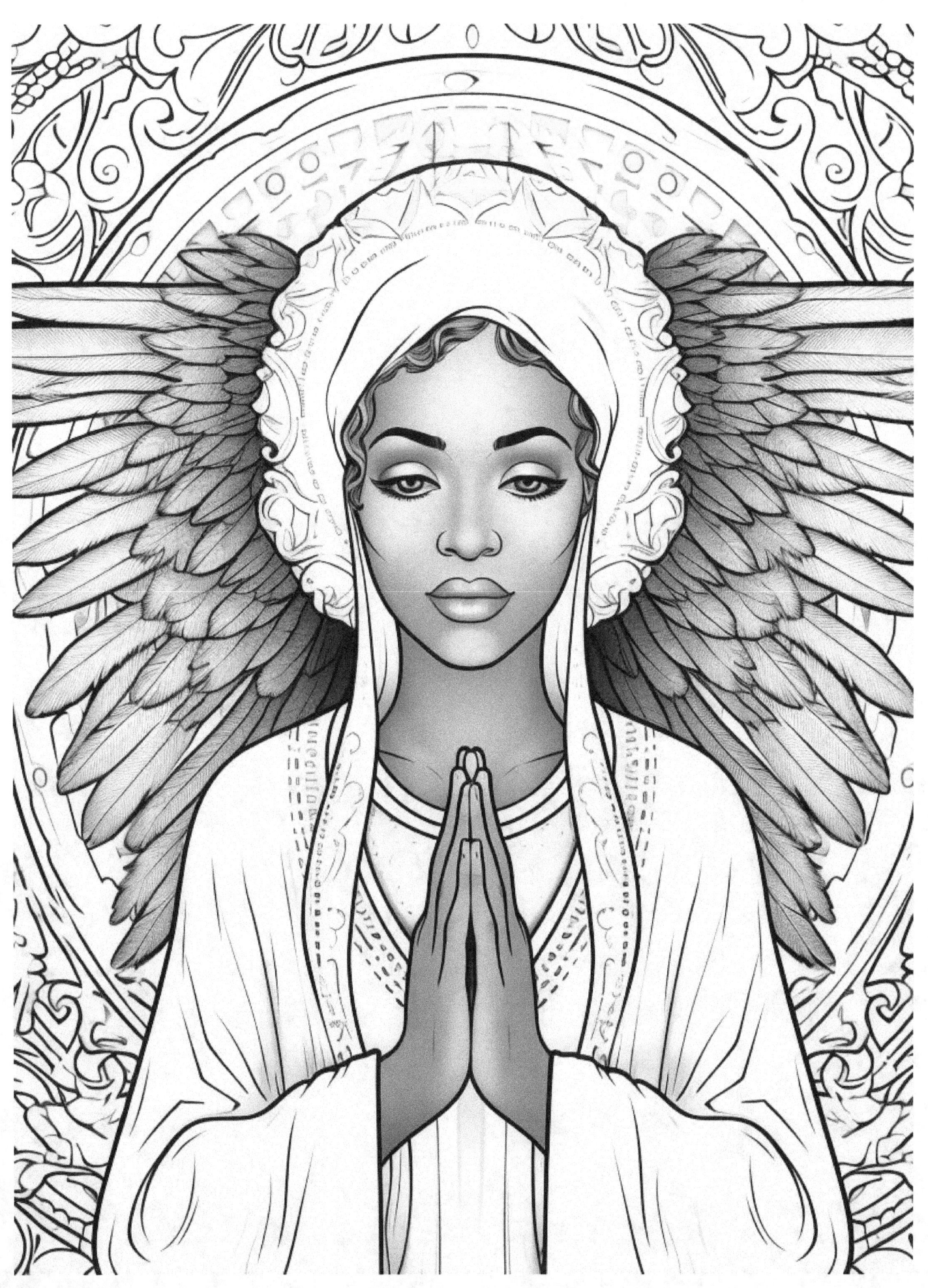

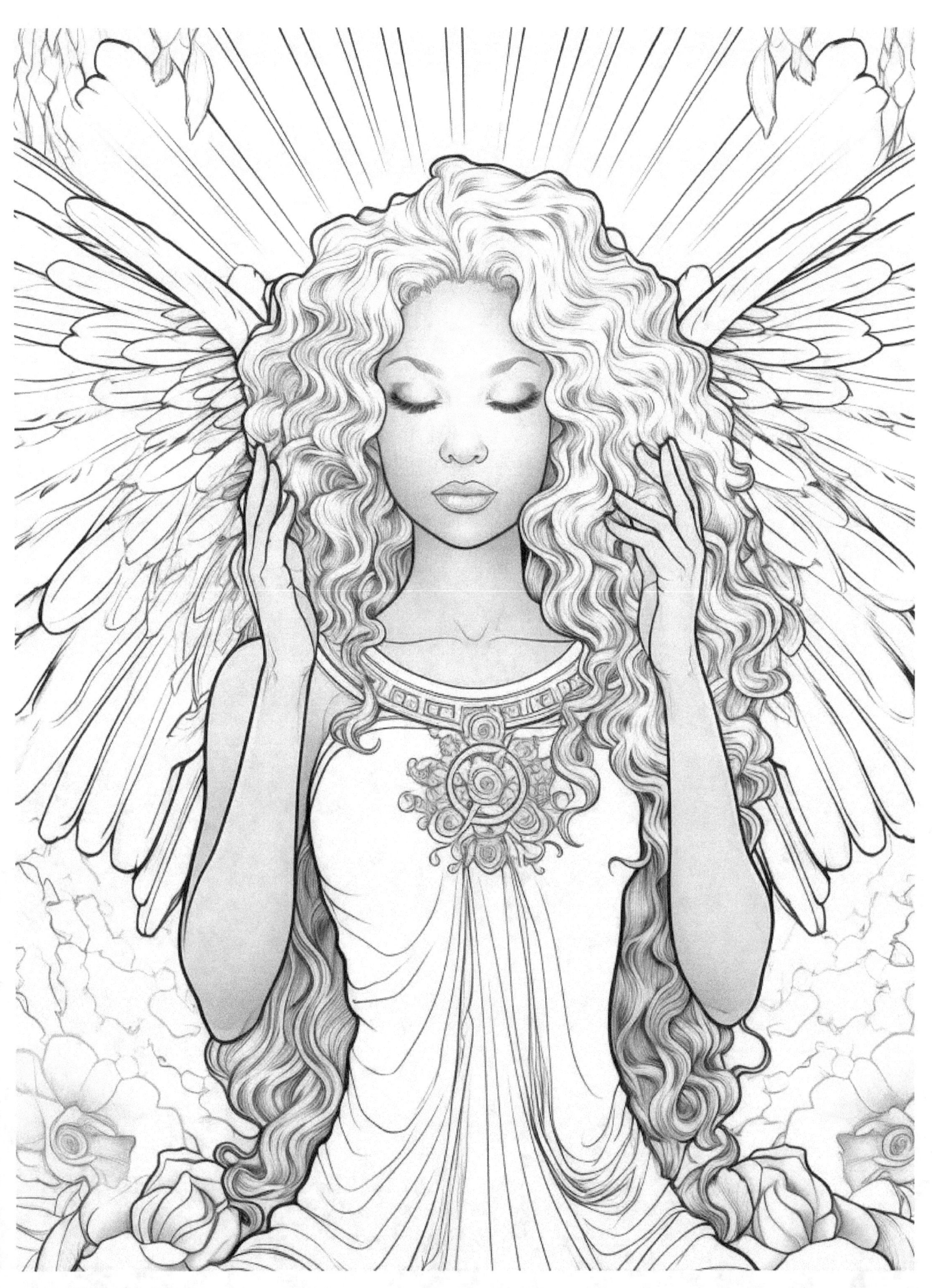

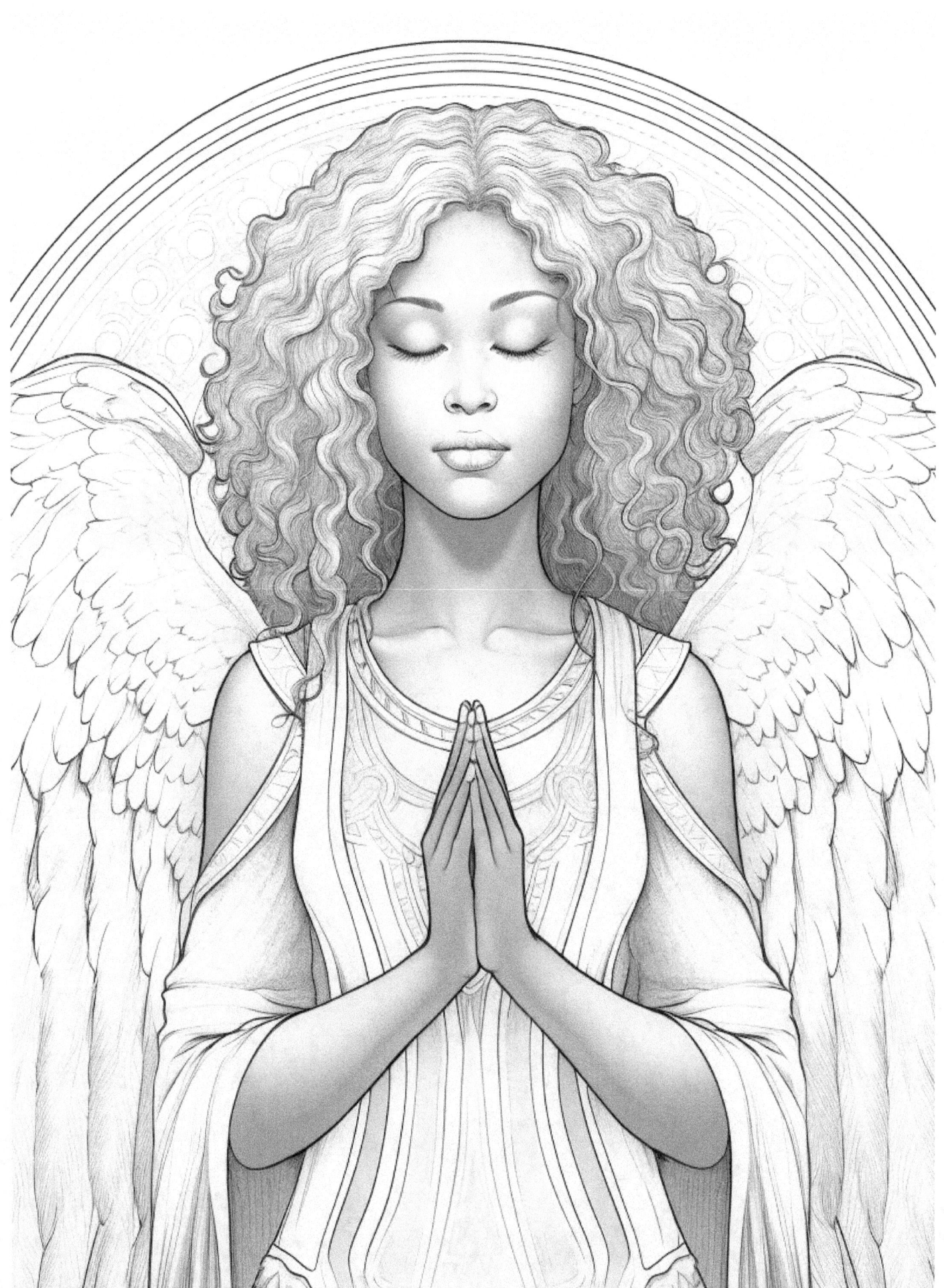

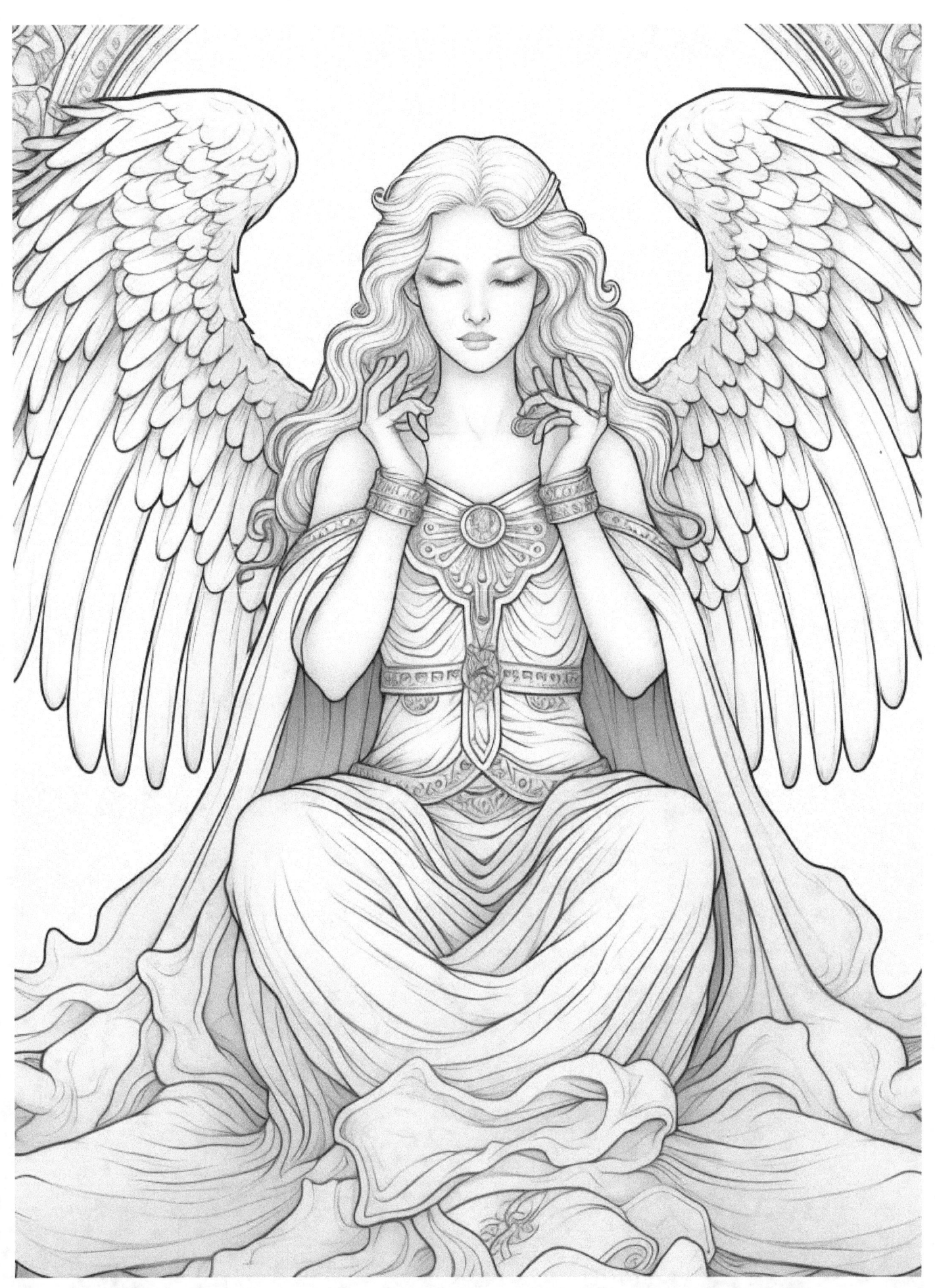

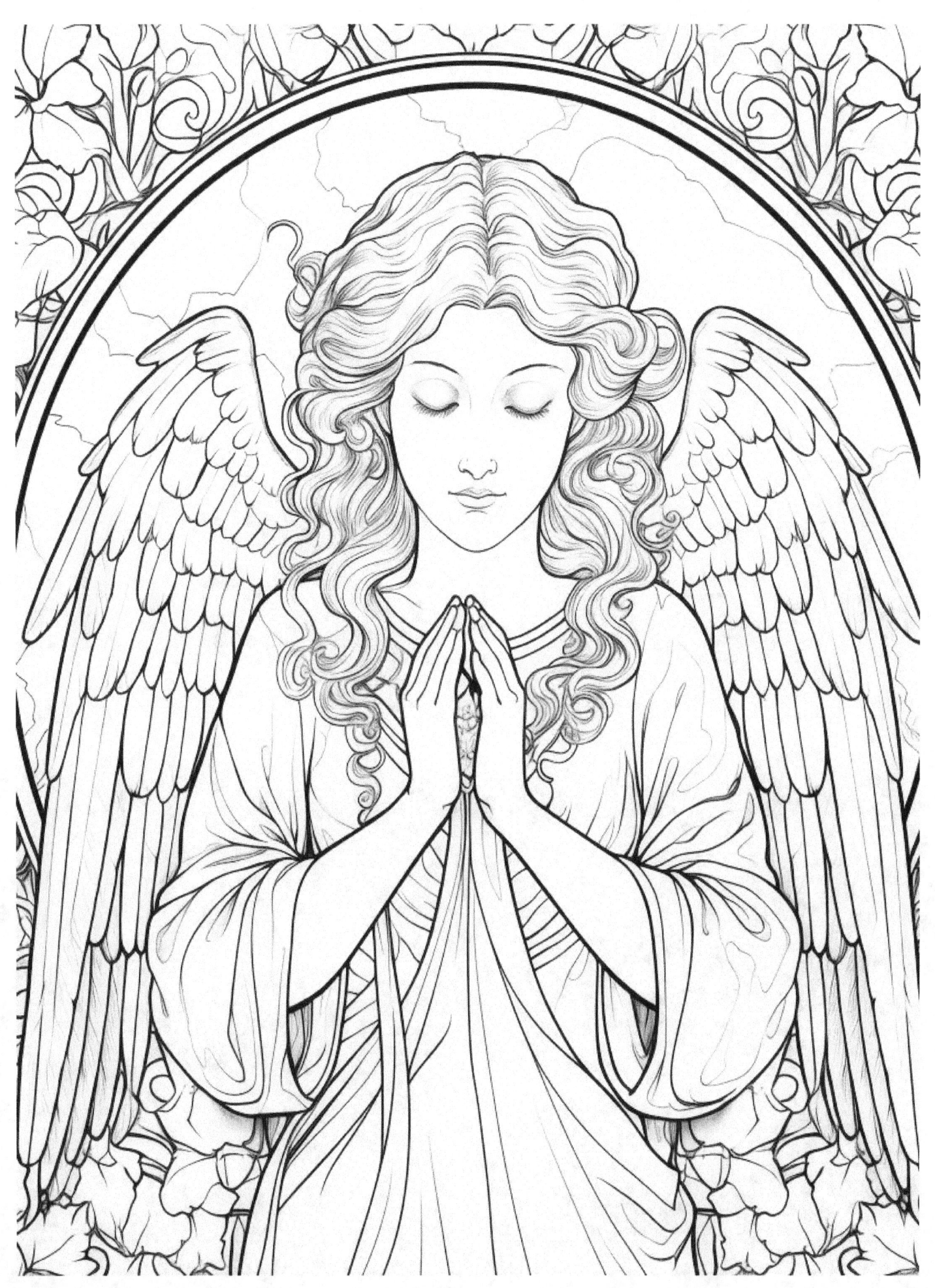

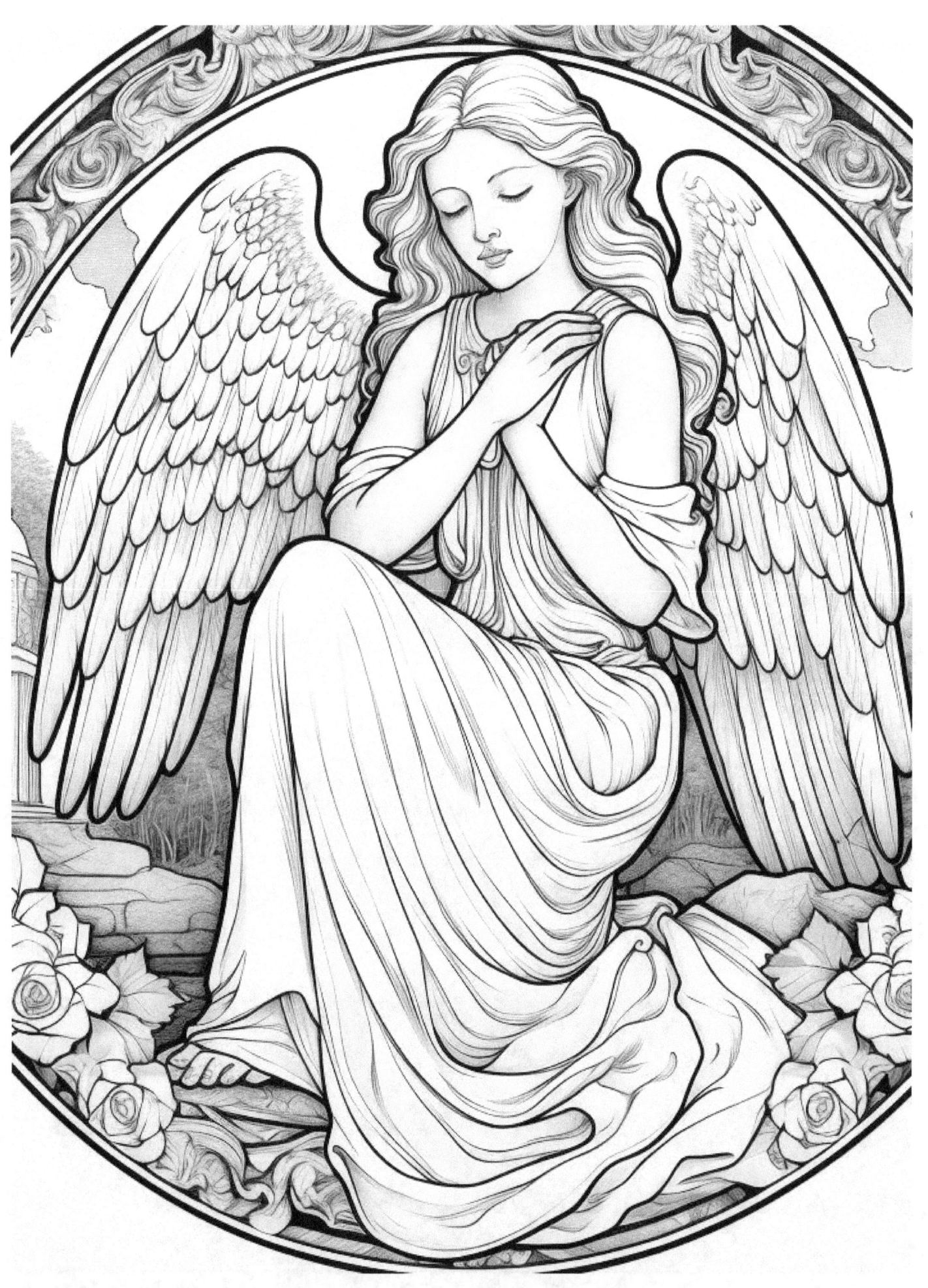

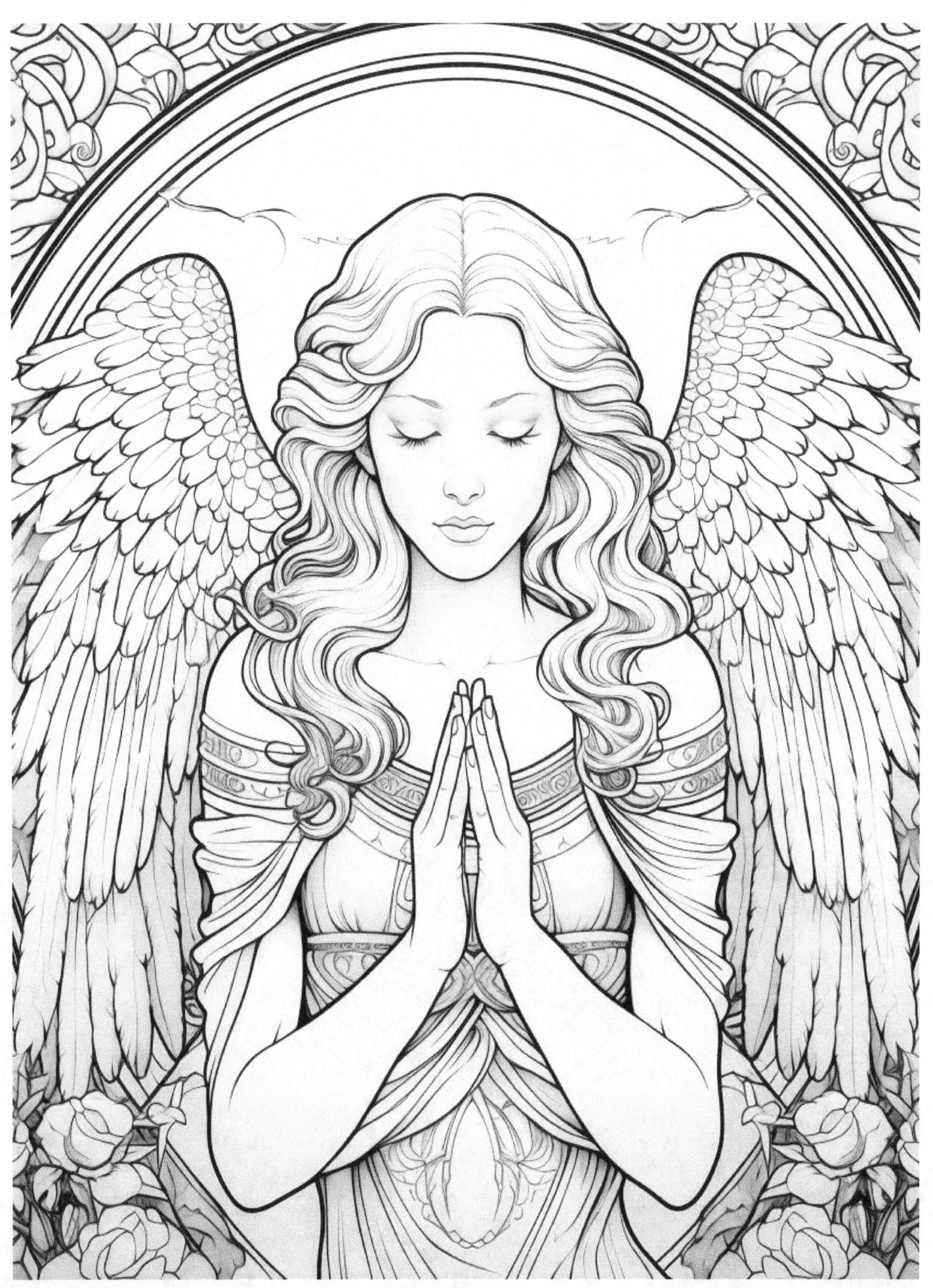

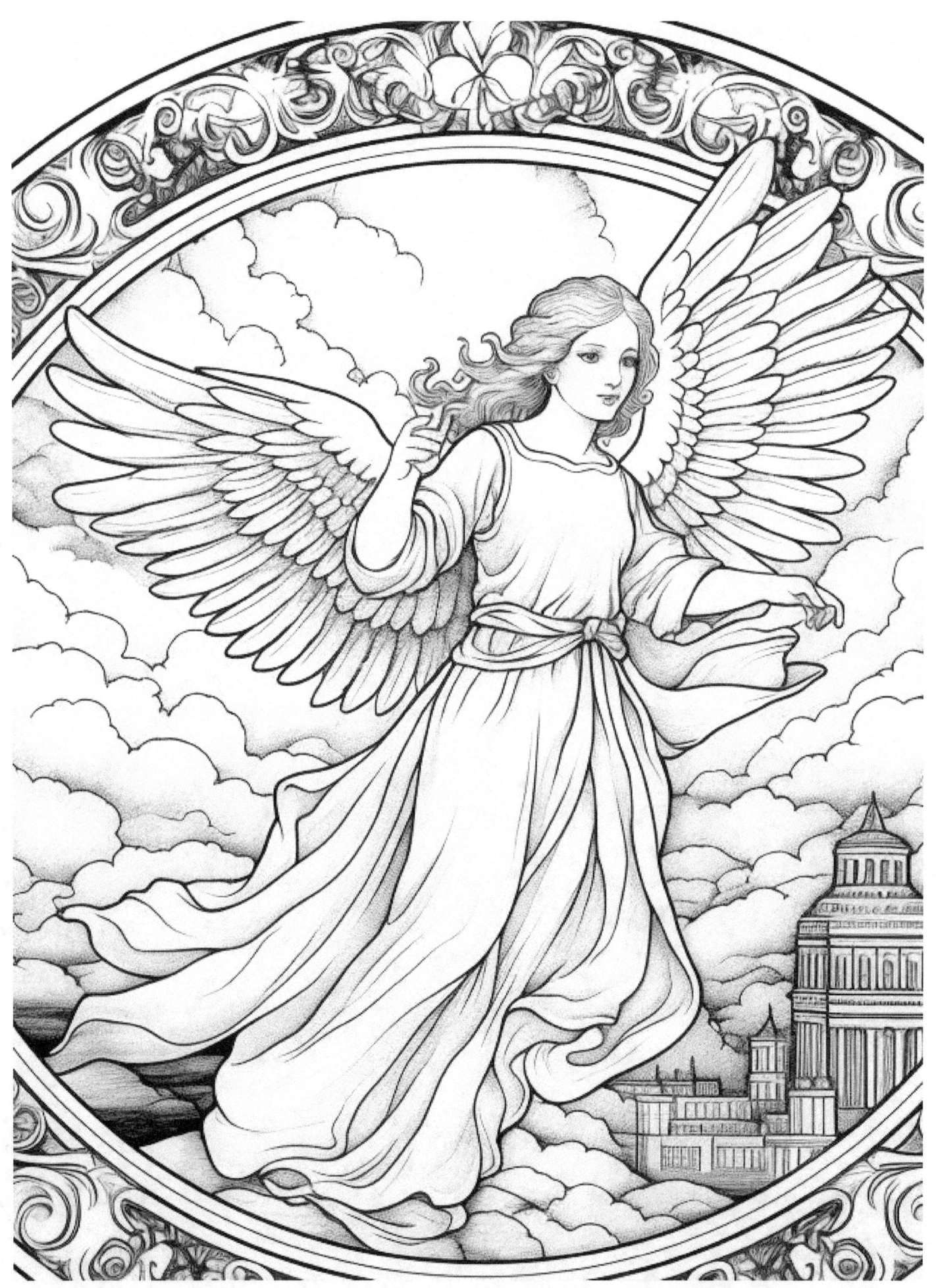

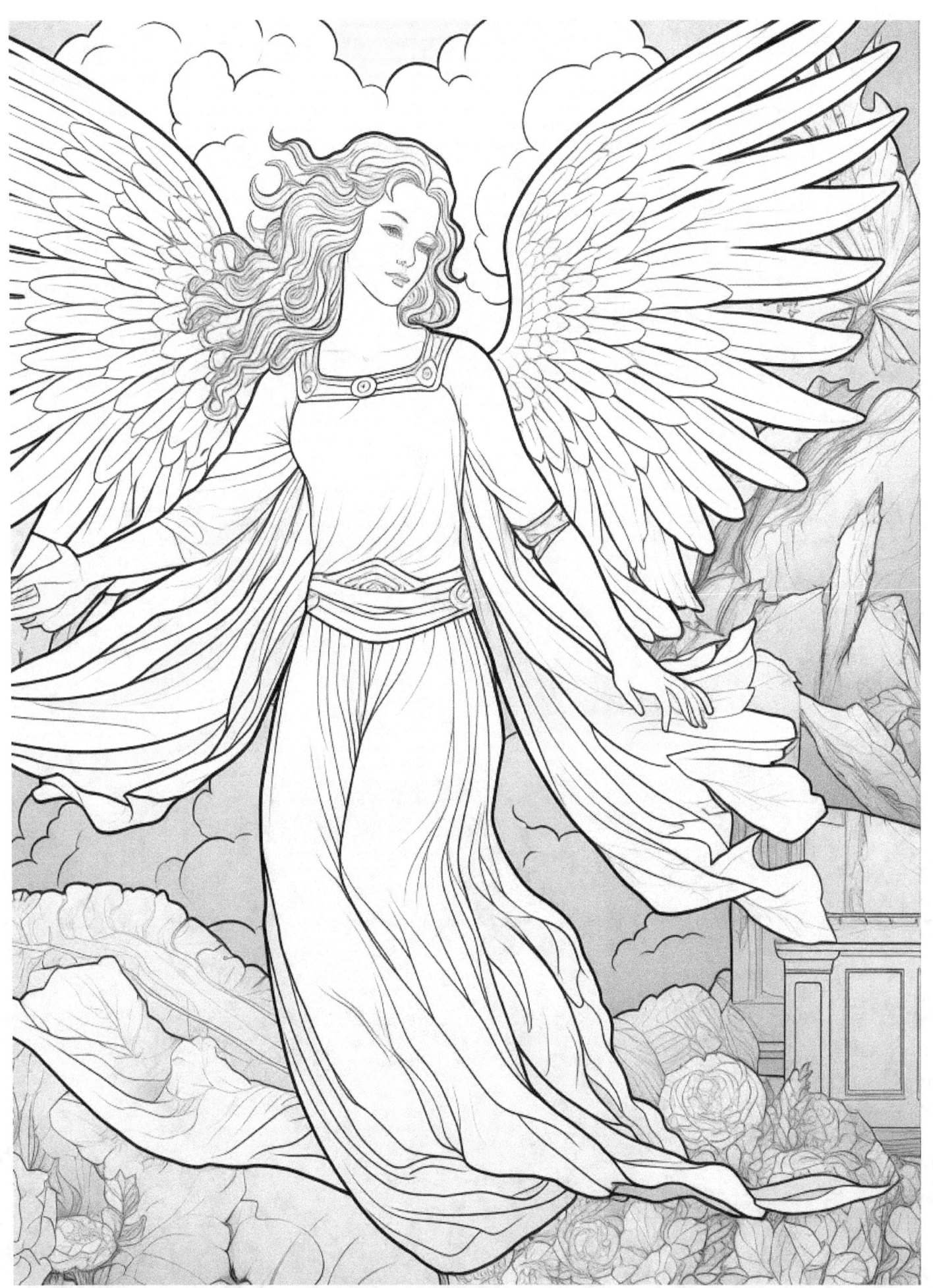

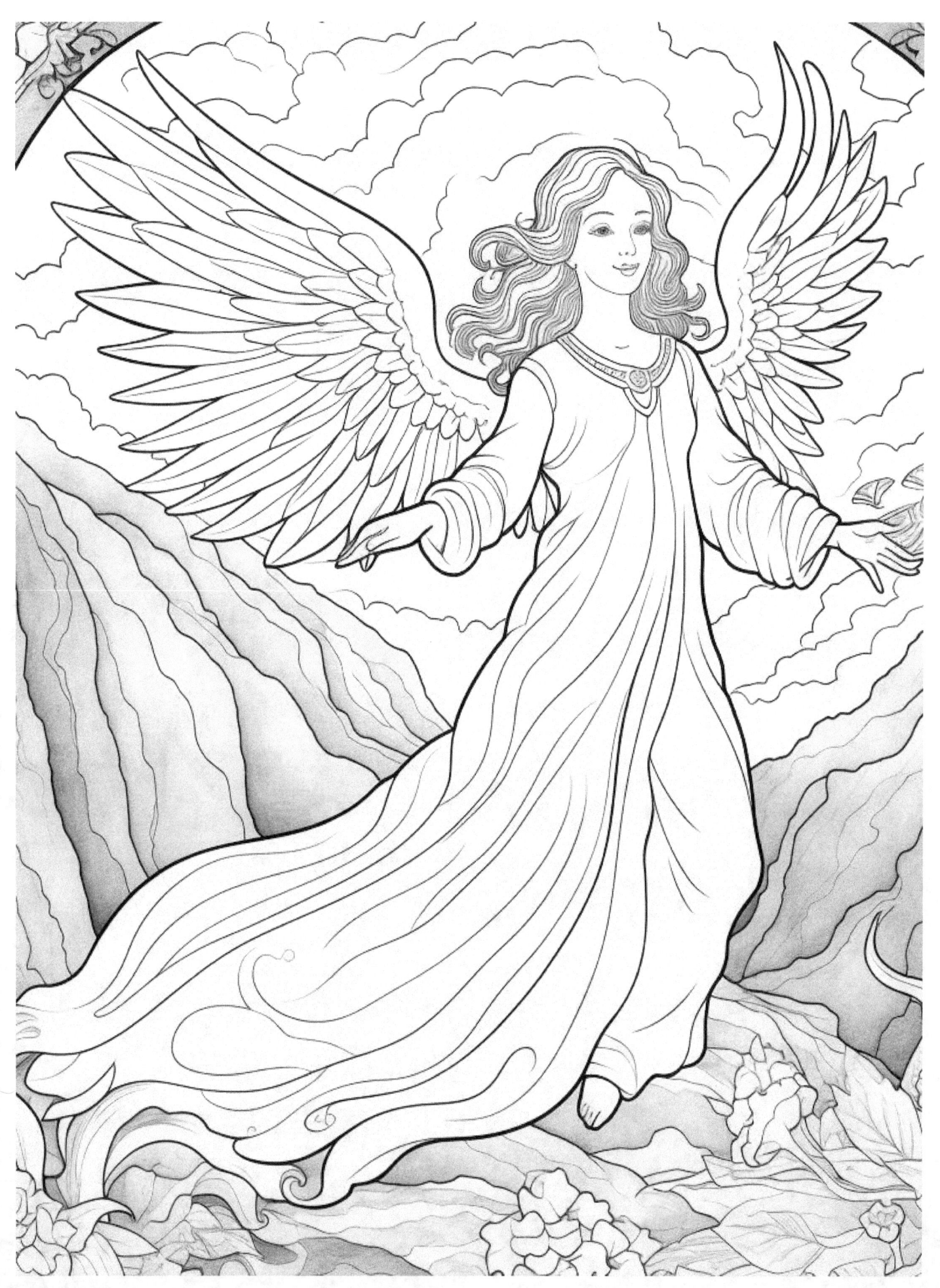

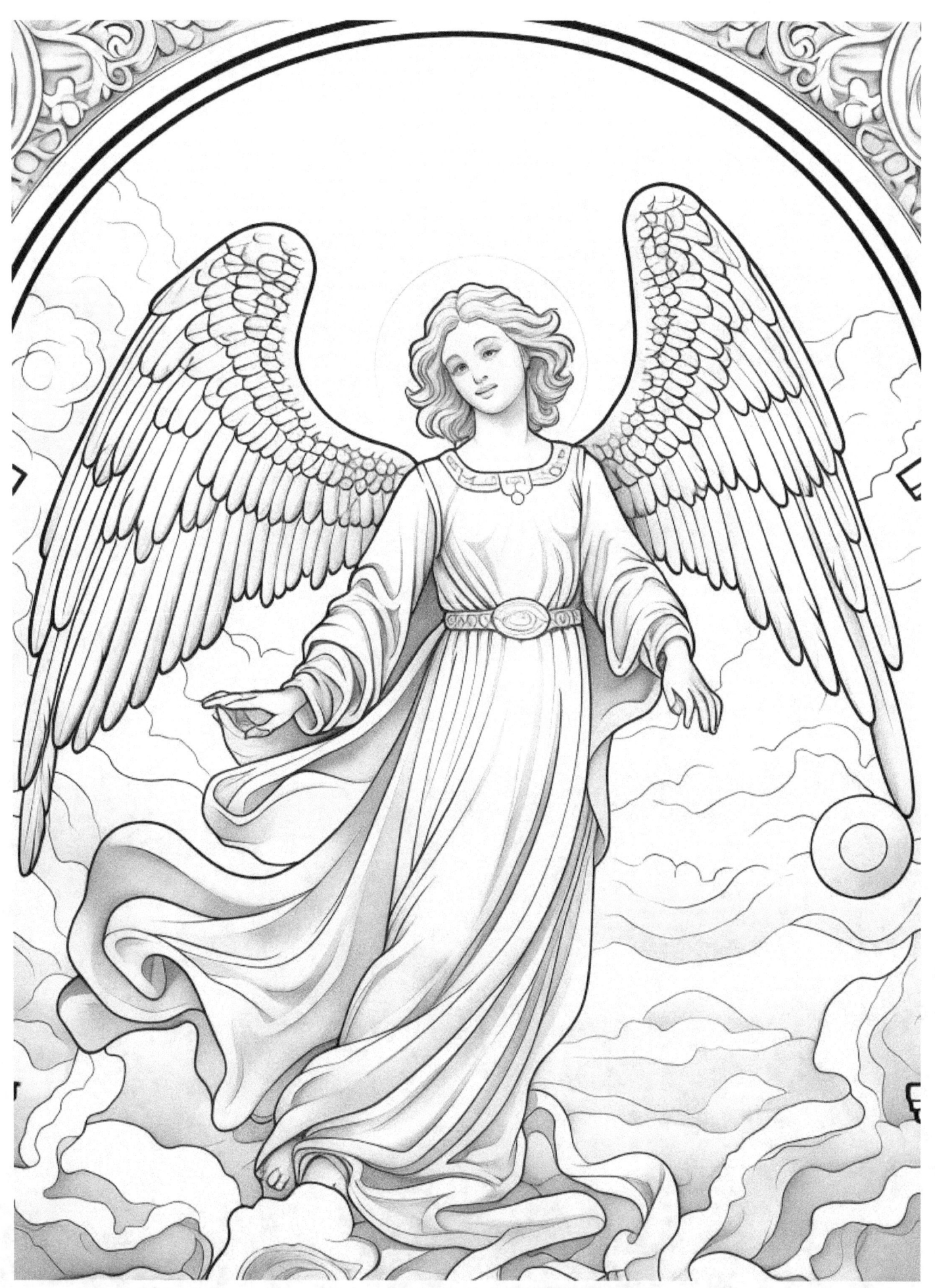

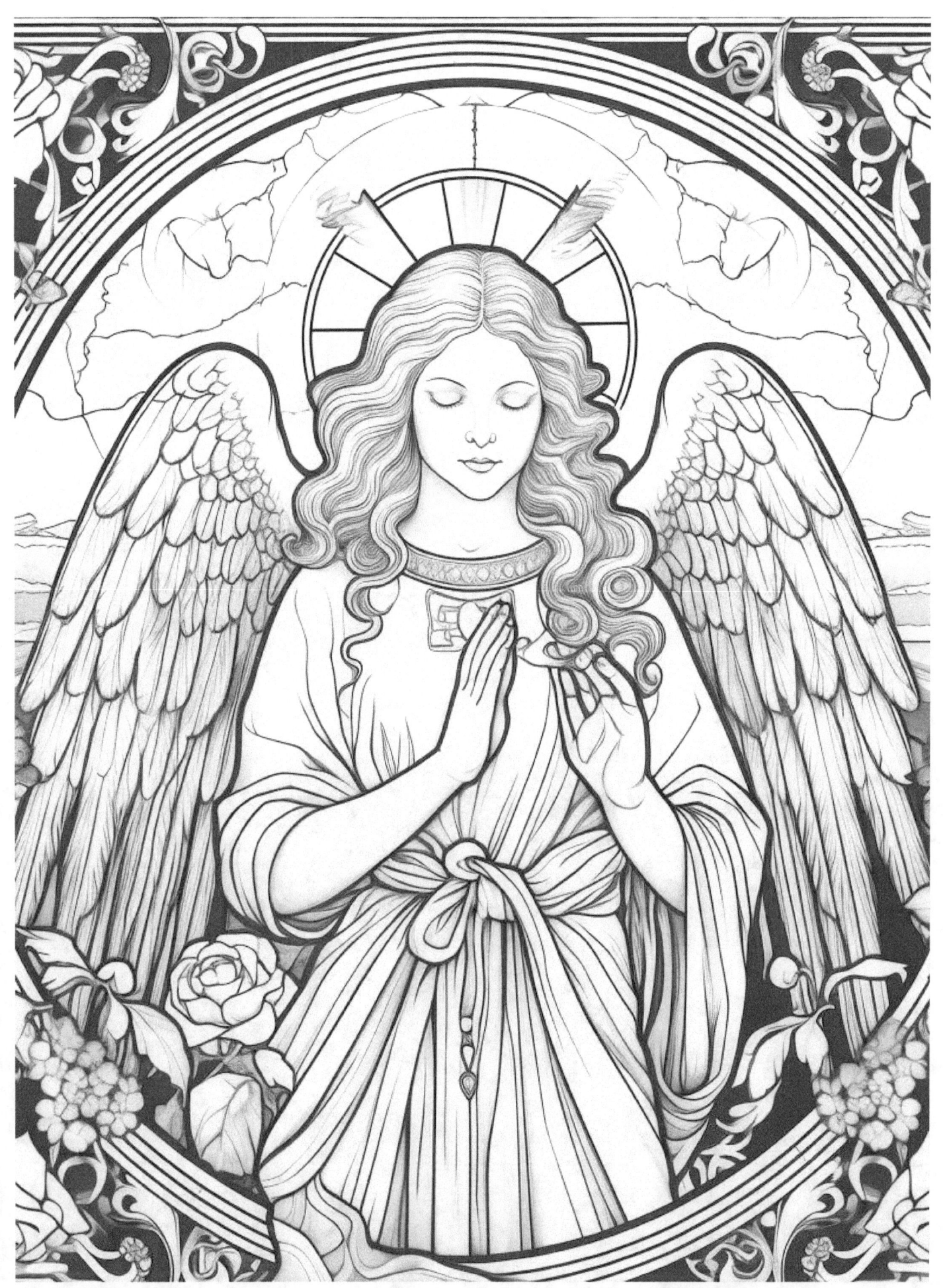

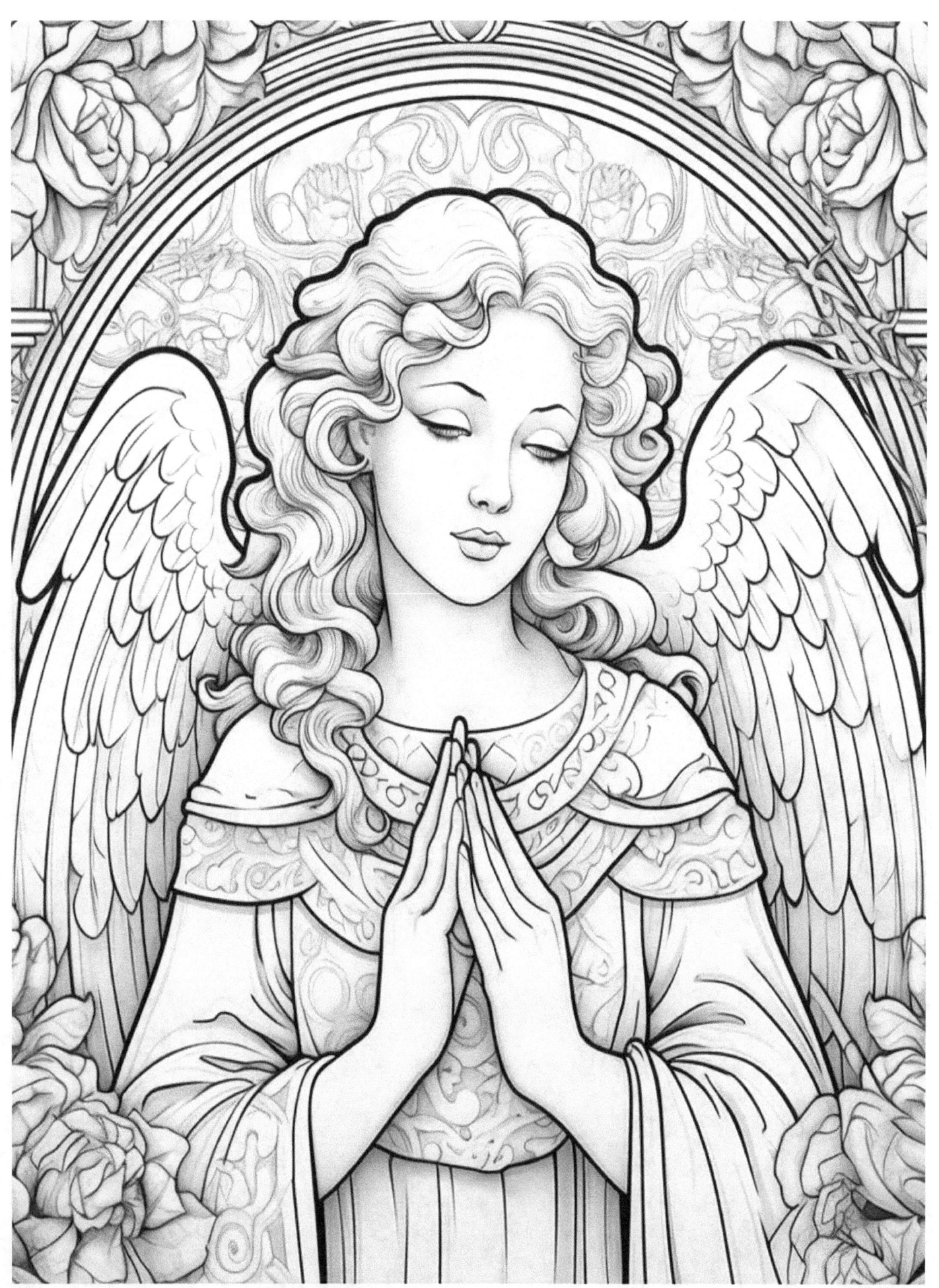

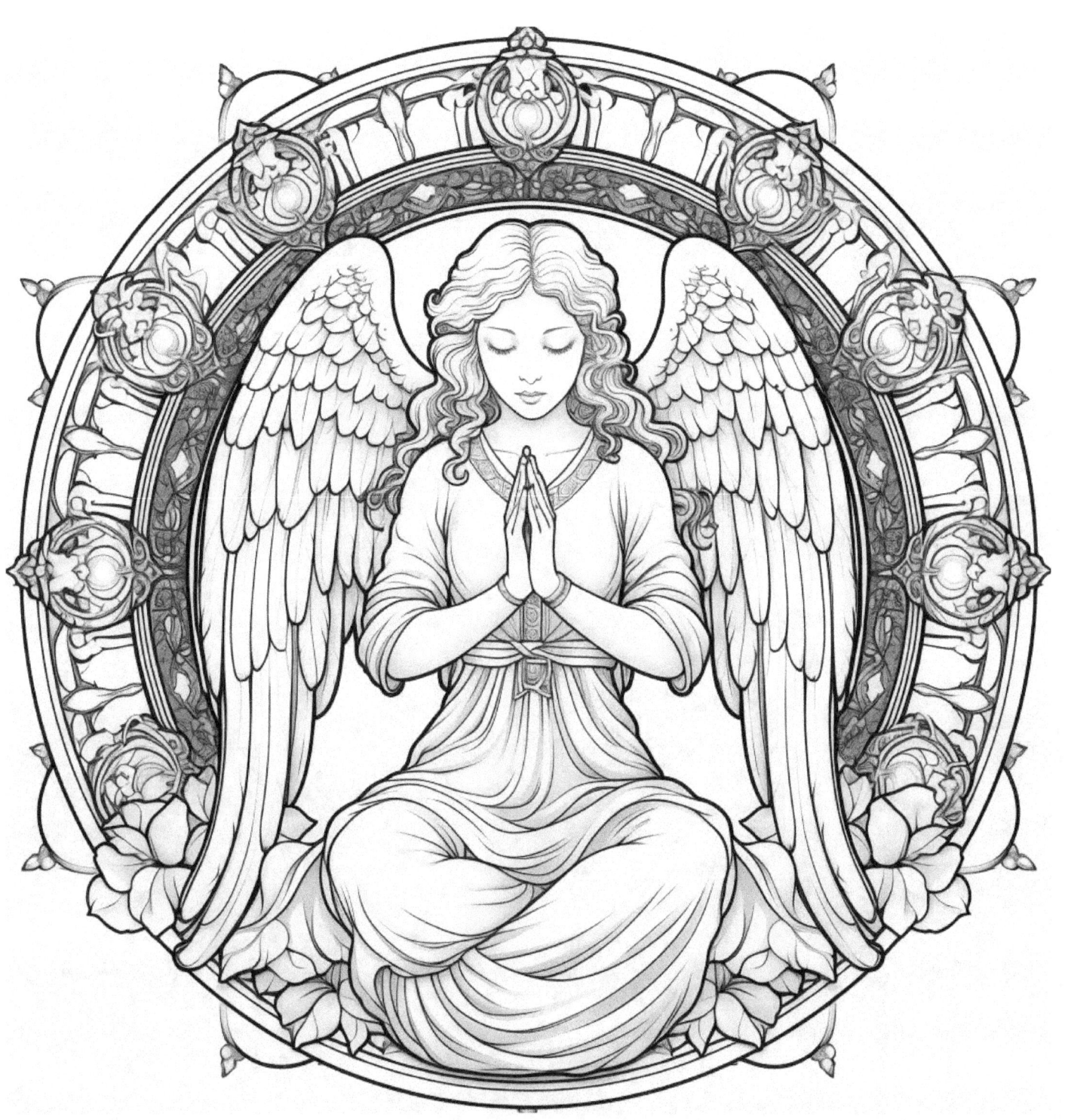

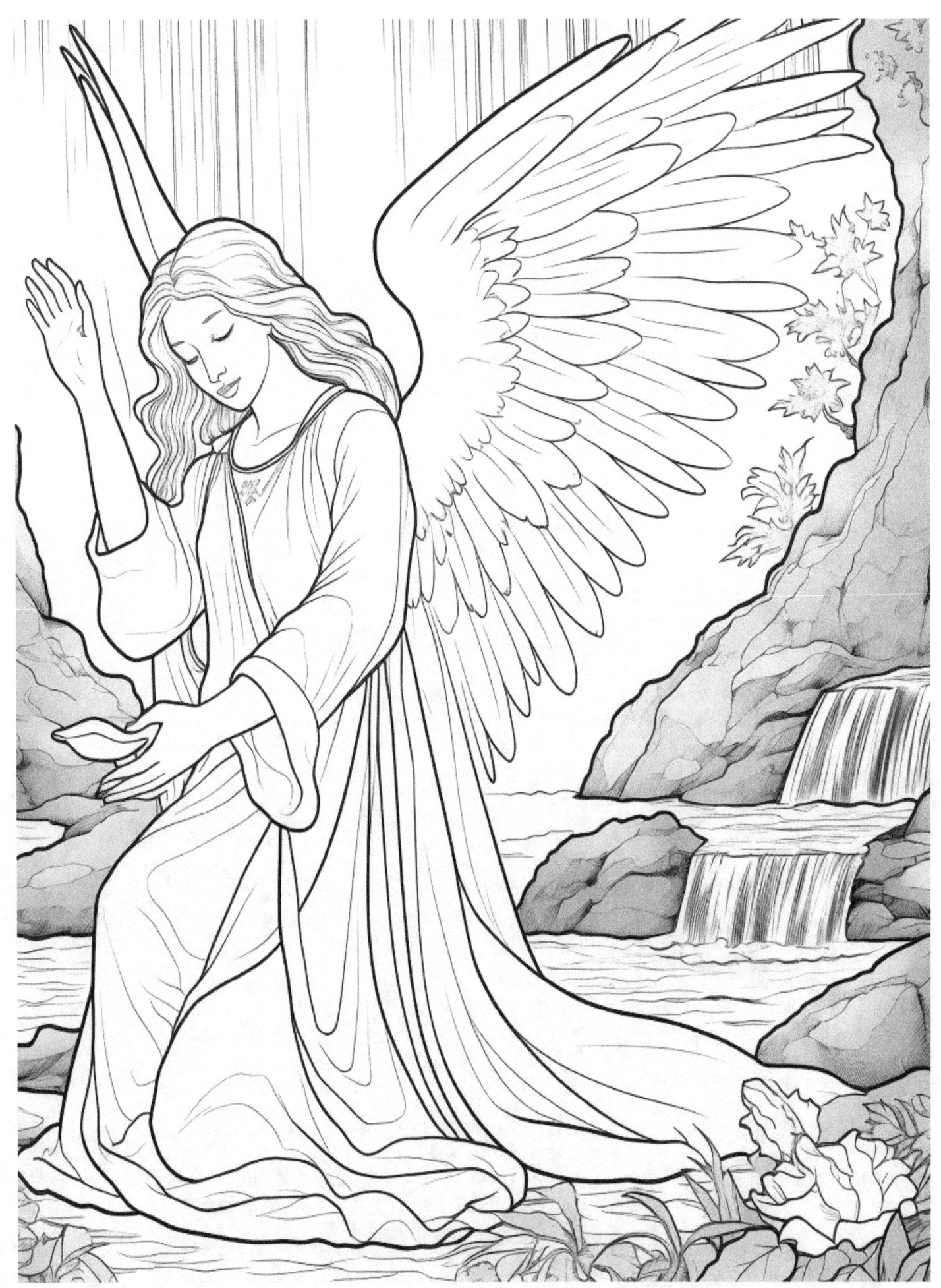

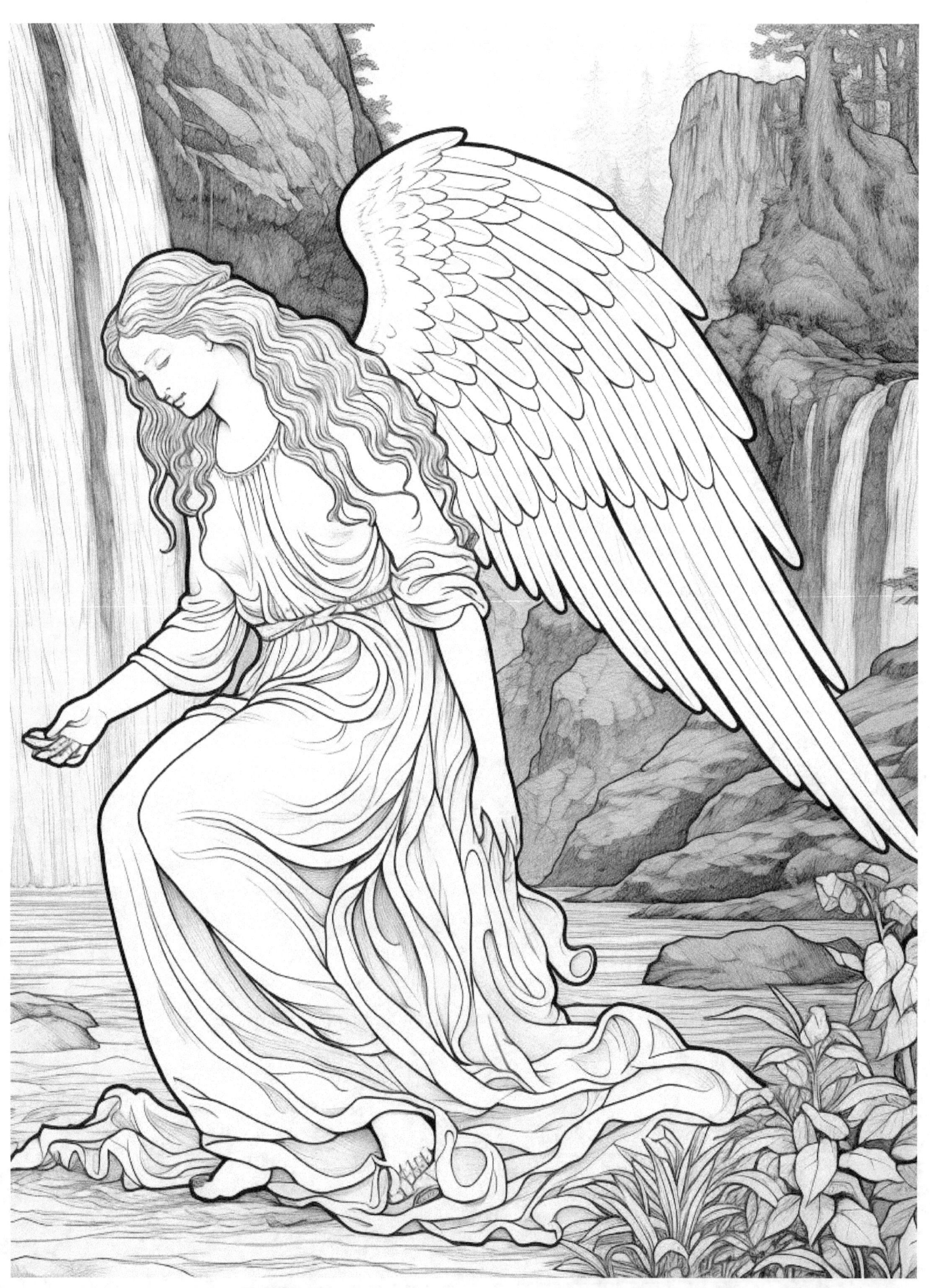

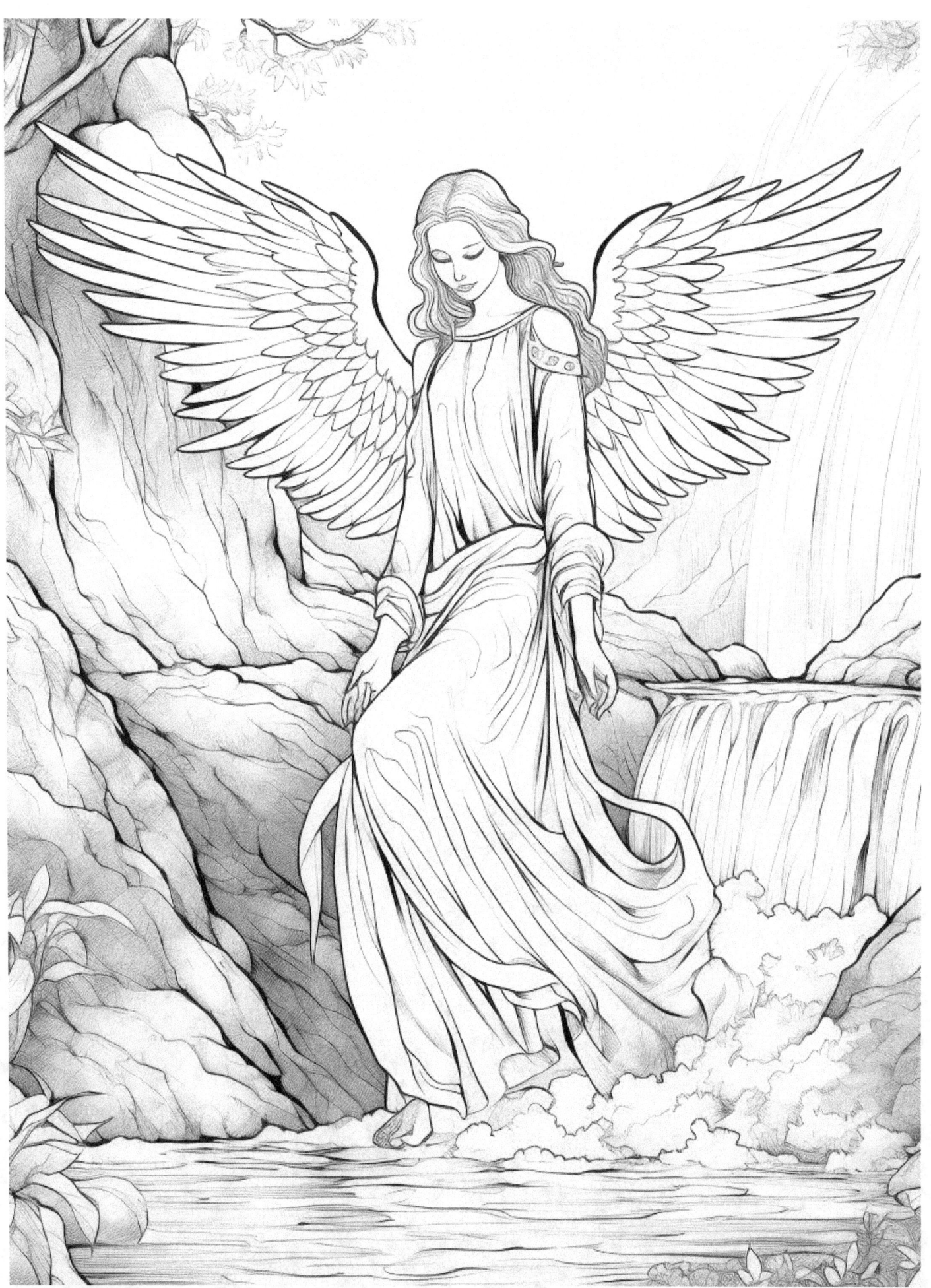

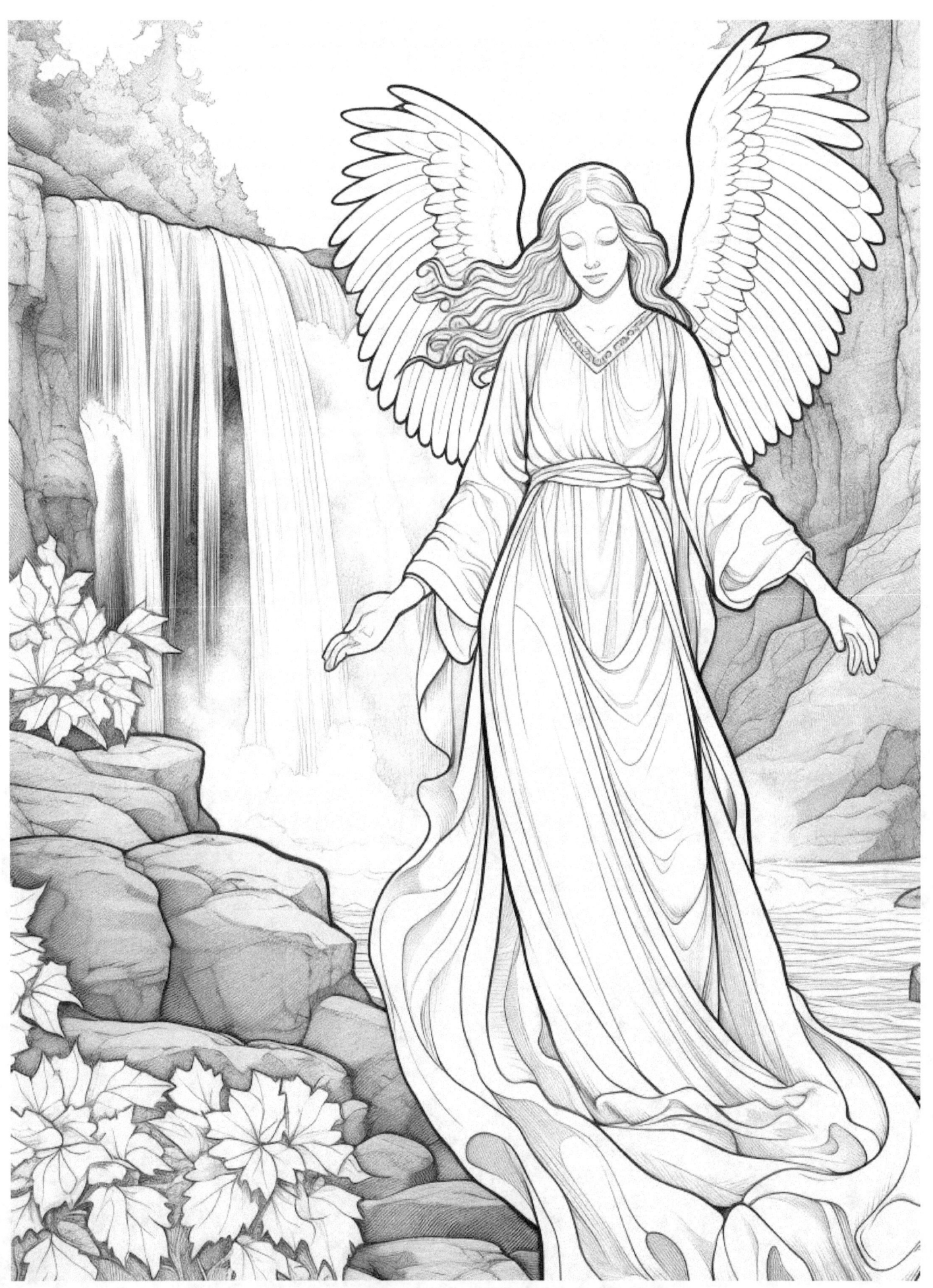

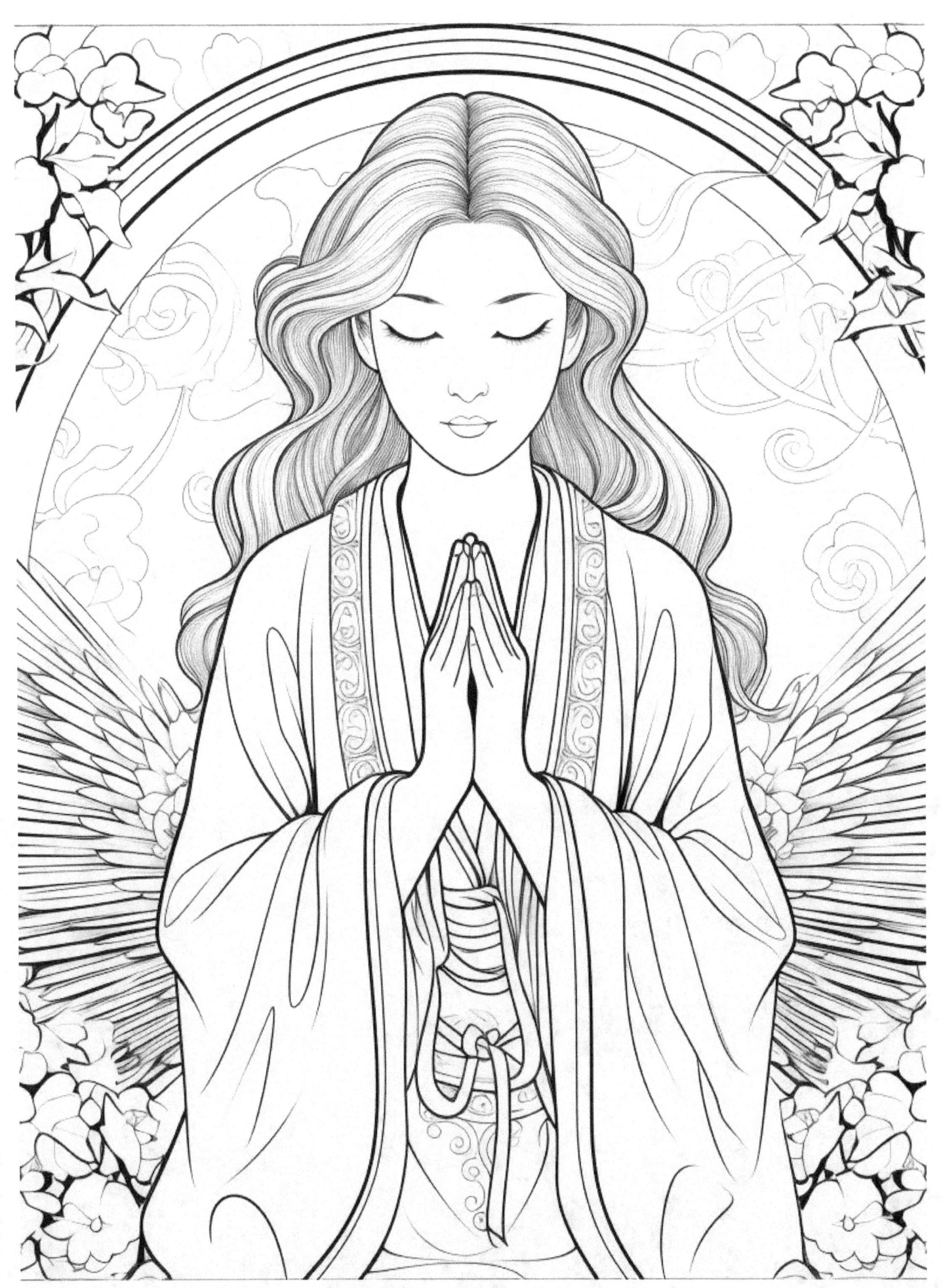

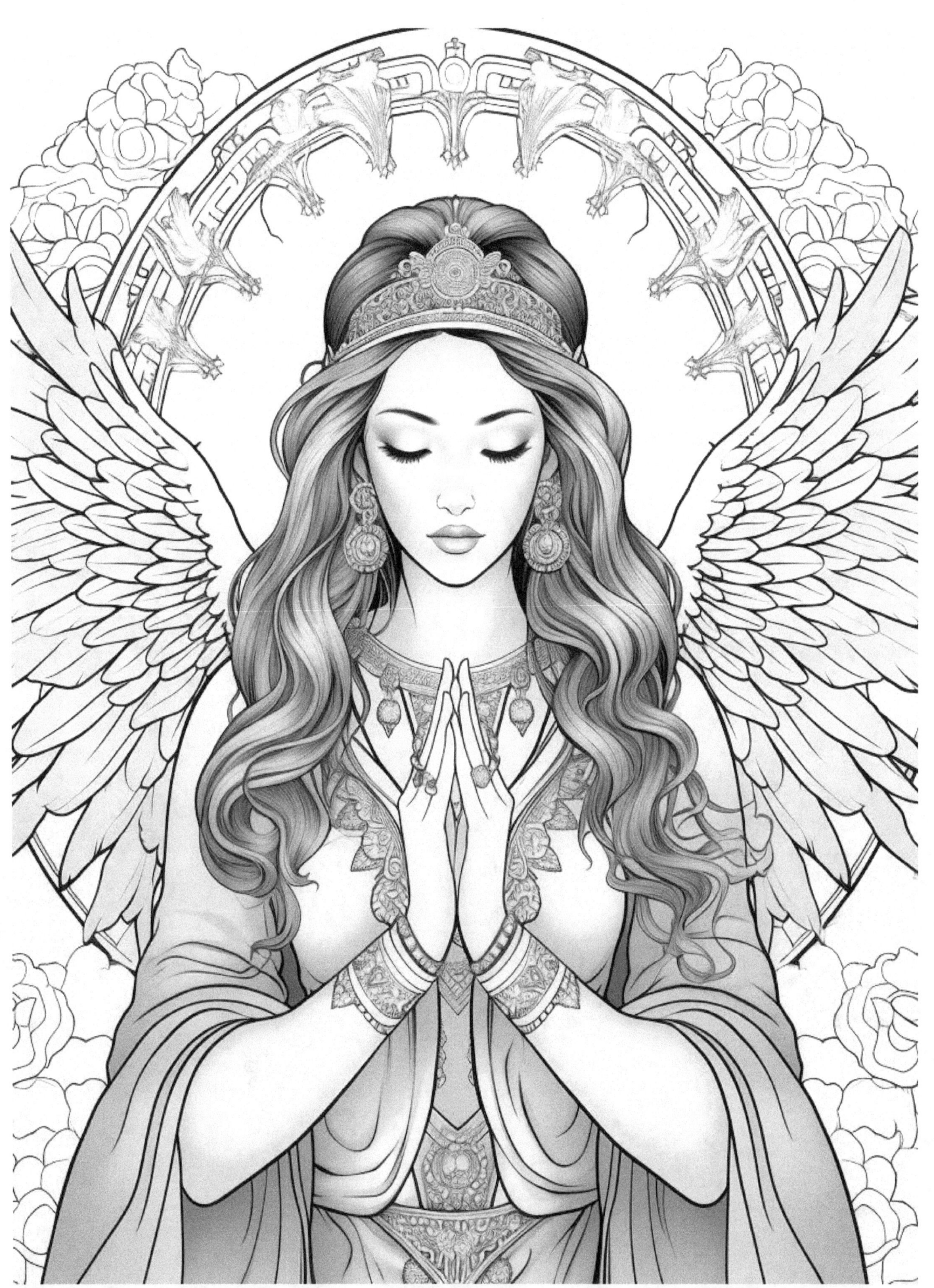

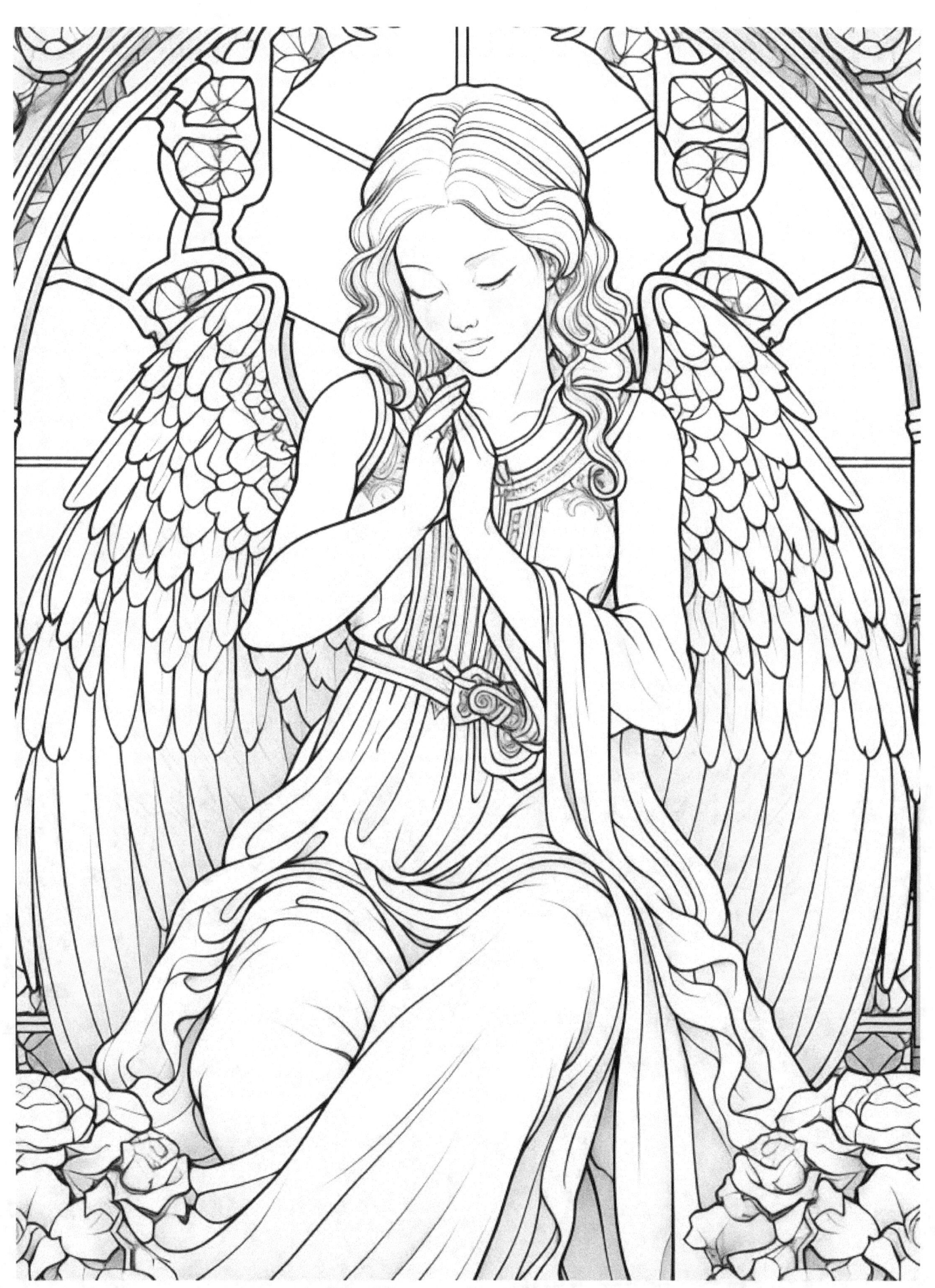

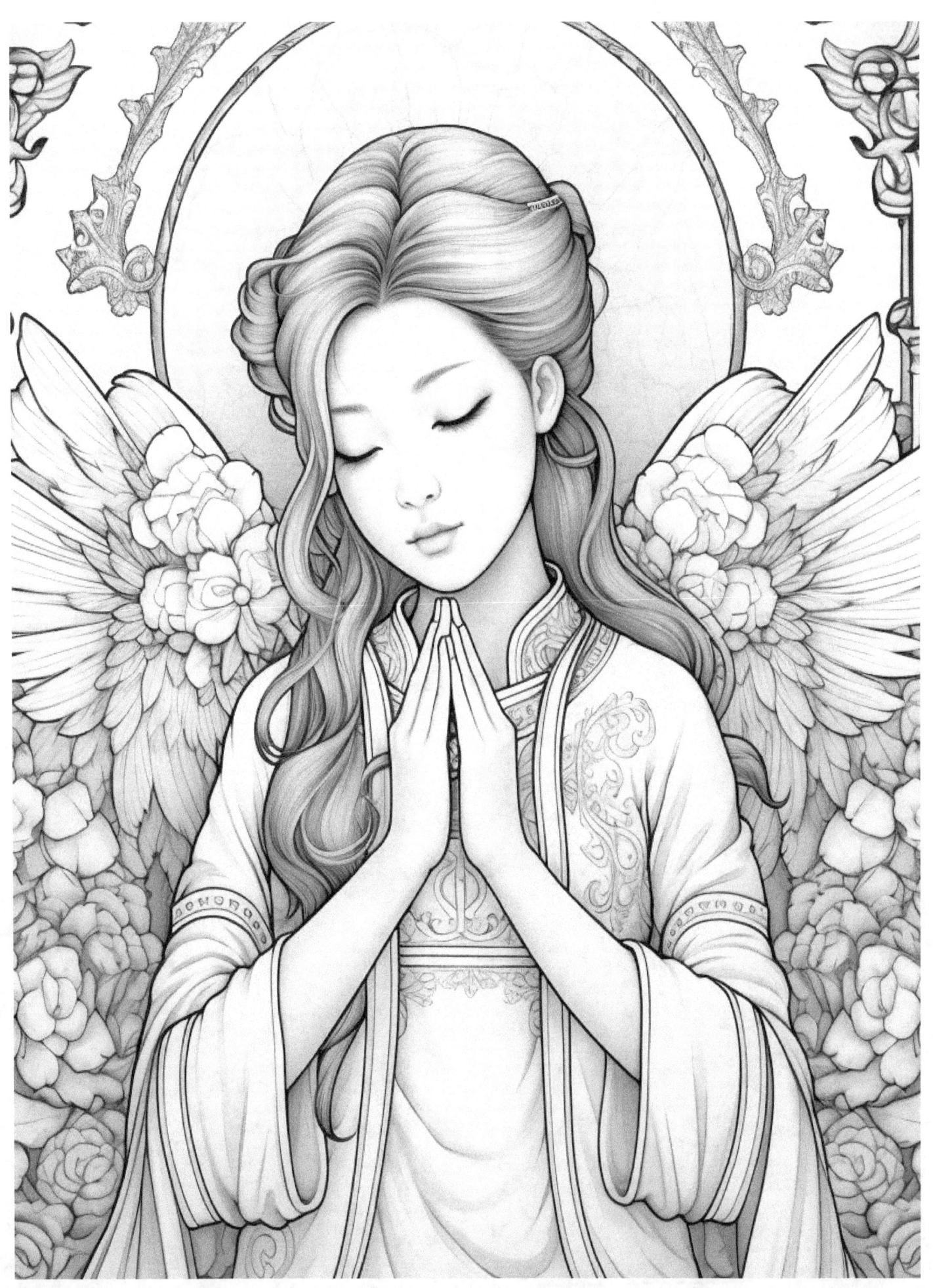

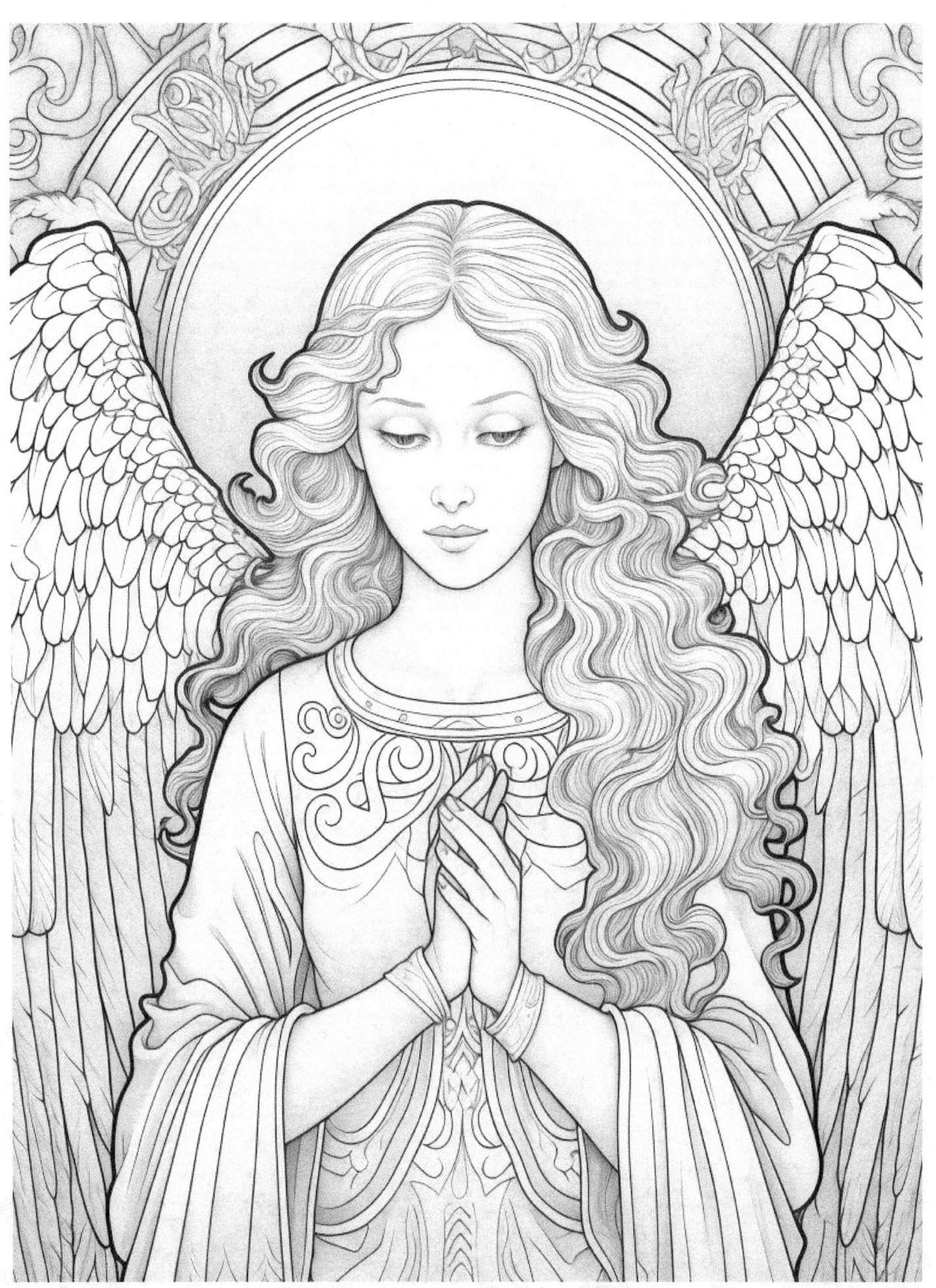

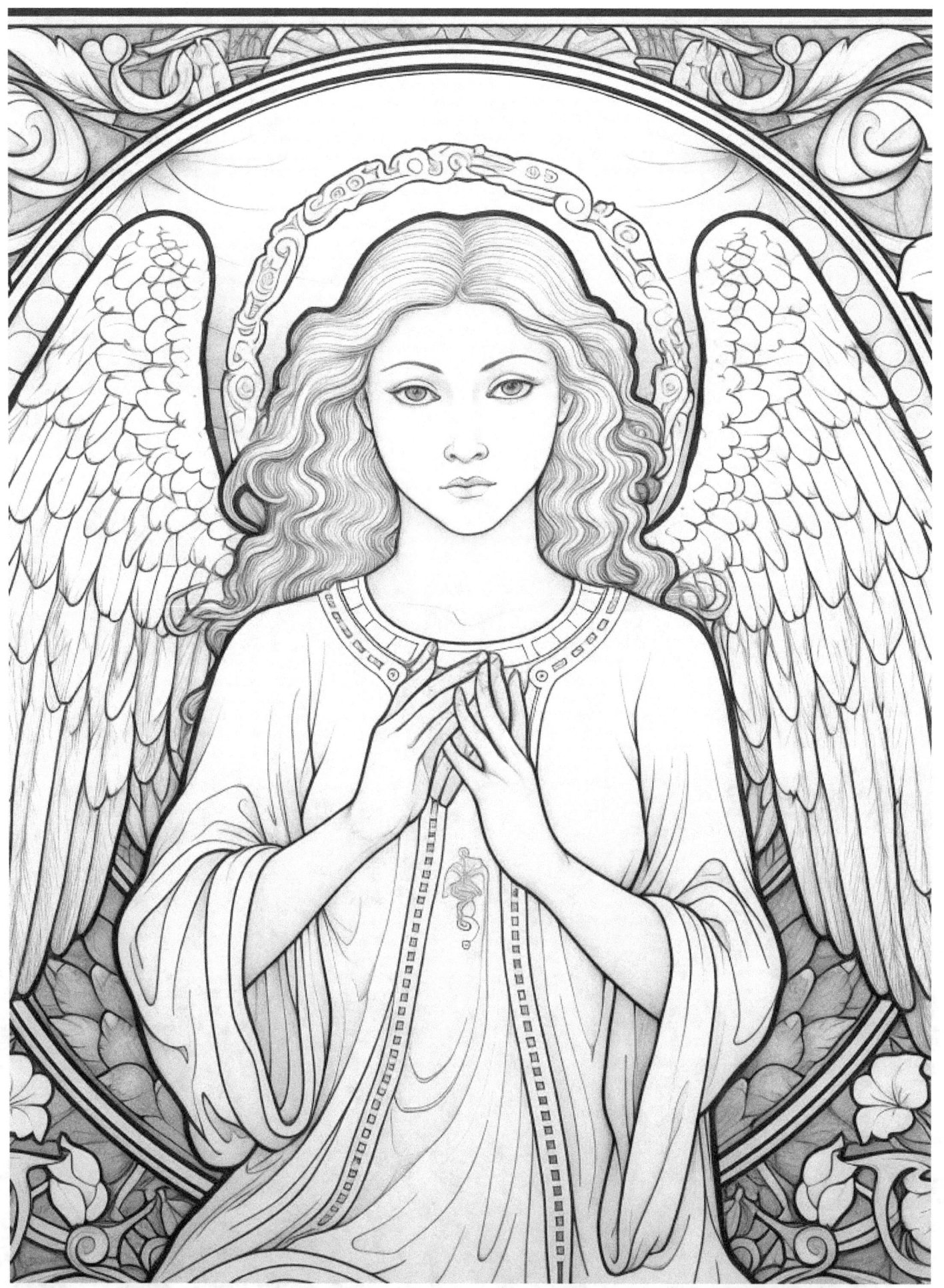

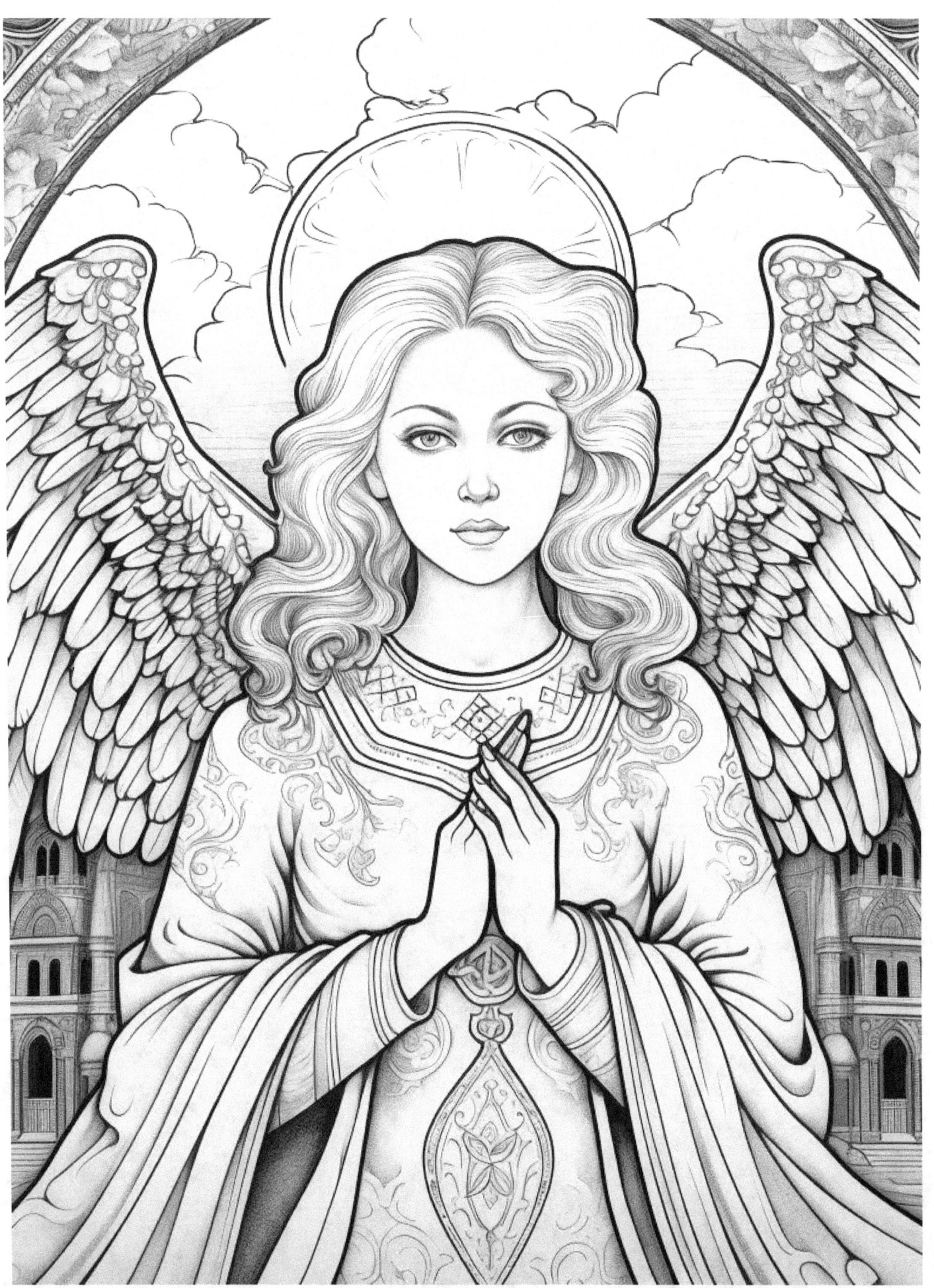

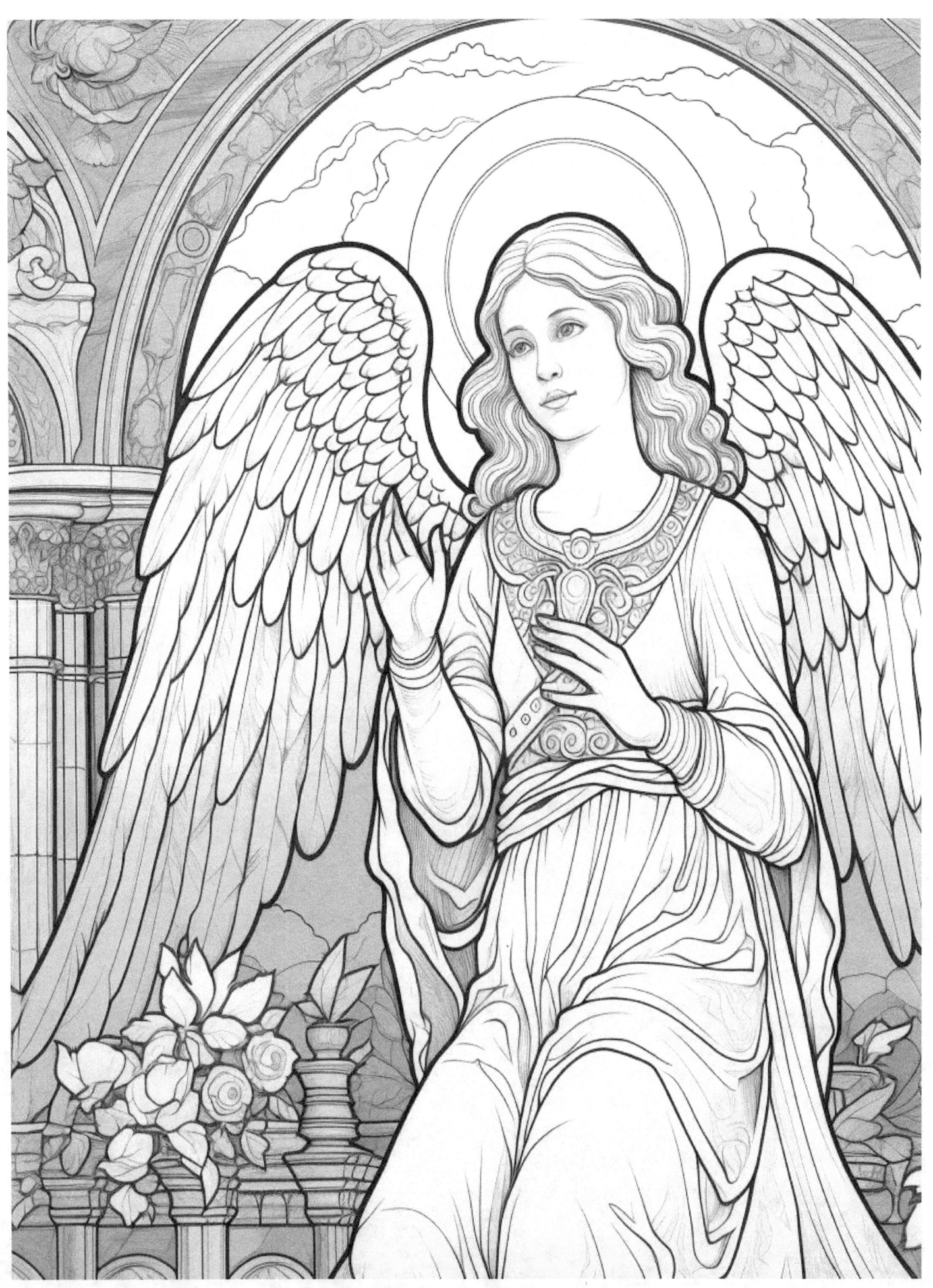

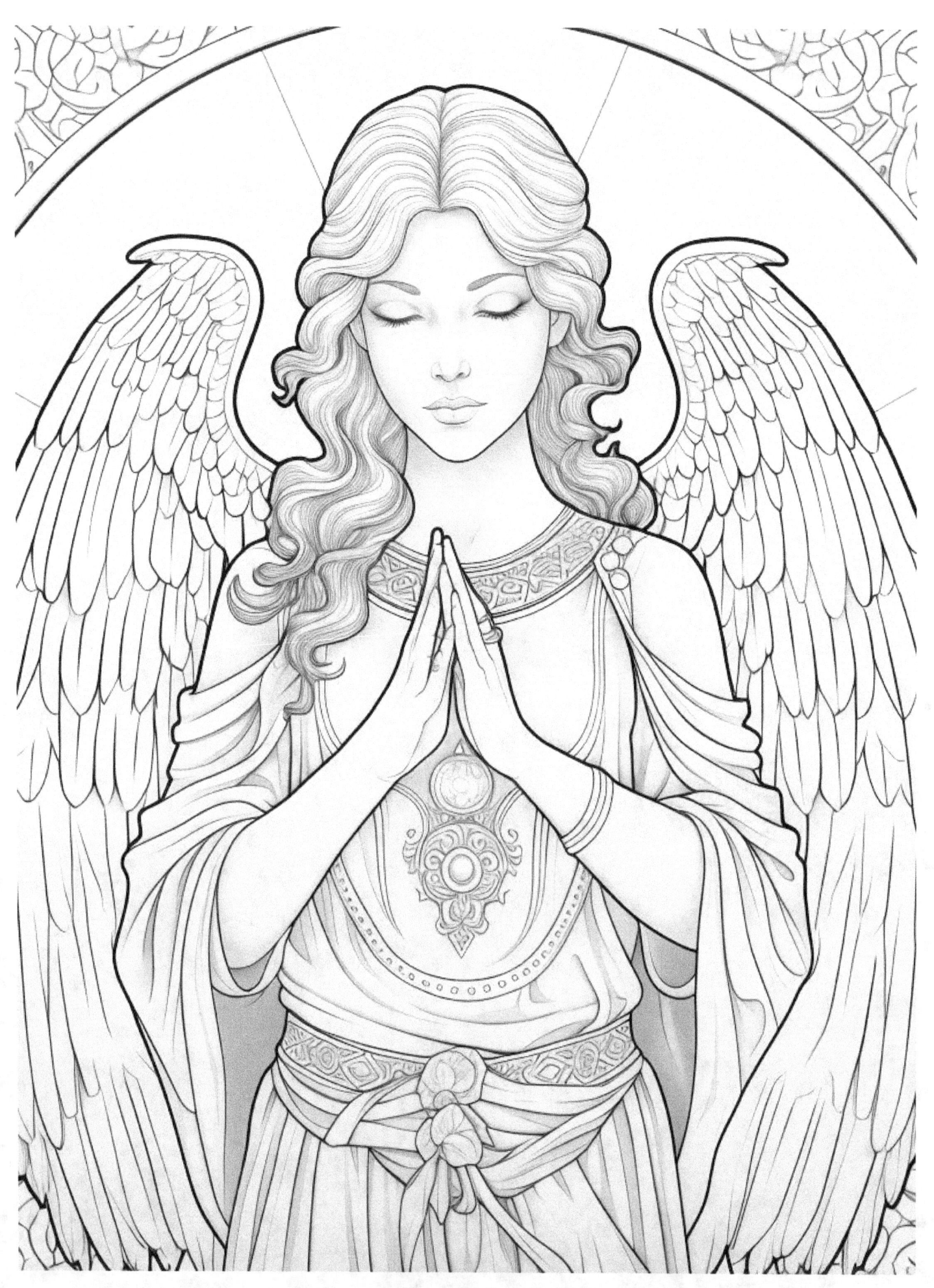

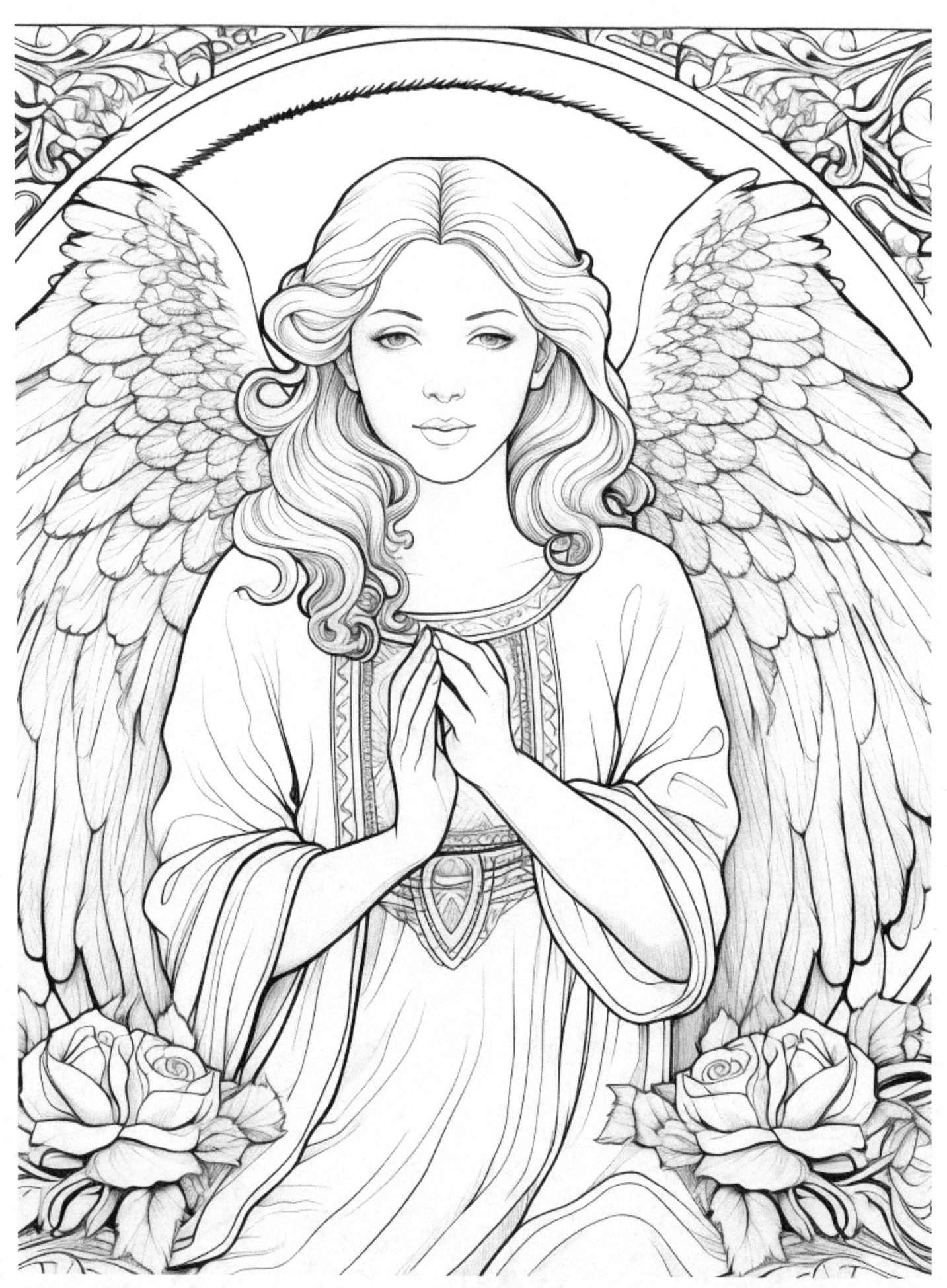

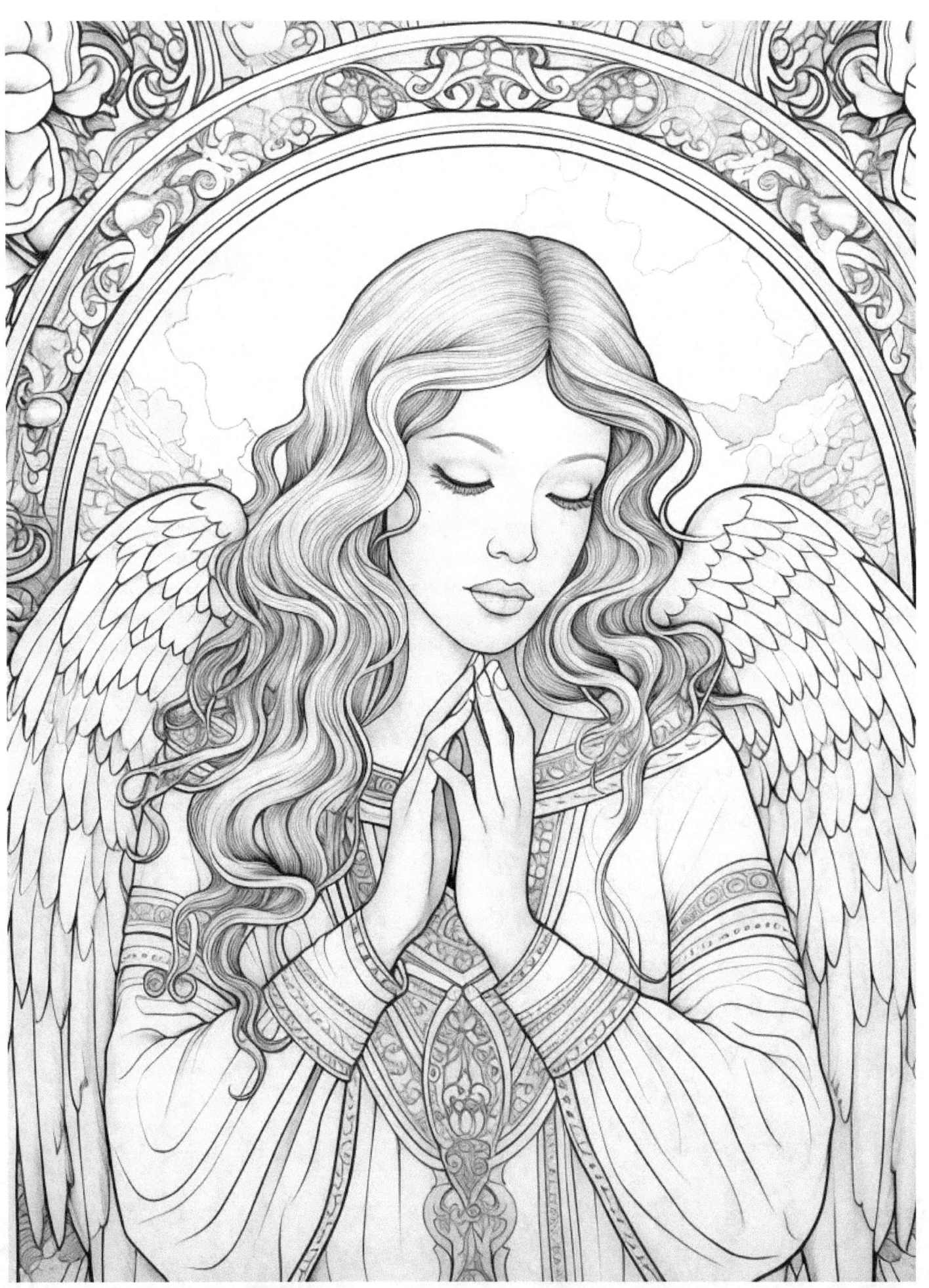

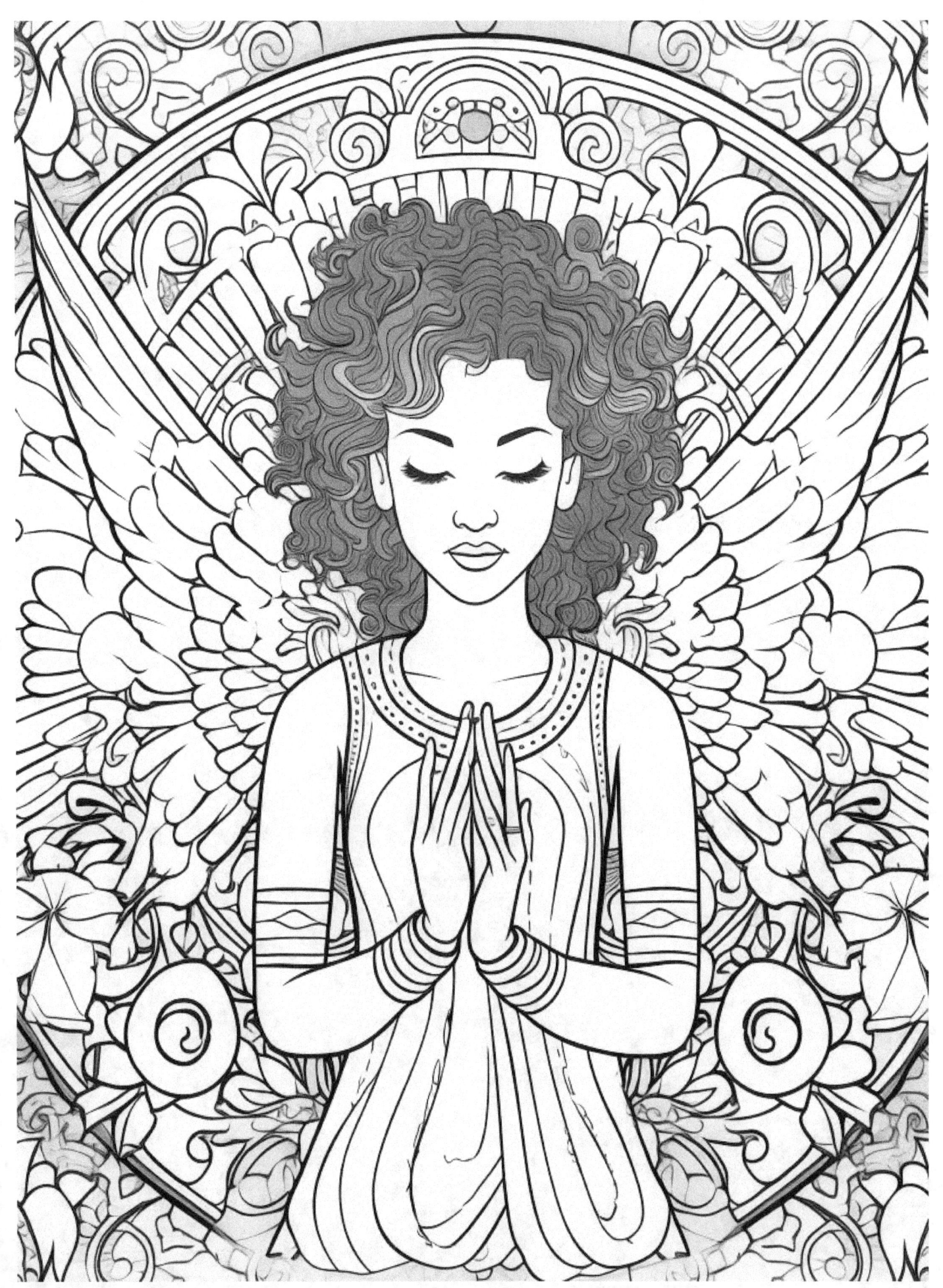